HOW TO PLAY

ROCK
GUITAR

LETHAL LICKS
& LESSONS!

FROM THE *GUITAR PLAYER* CHOP SHOP

BY THE EDITORS OF

GuitarPlayer ®

 **Miller Freeman Books**

SAN FRANCISCO

INTRODUCTION

Whether you're a beginner or professional, *How To Play Rock Guitar* is packed with tips, lessons, licks, and music that can improve your playing right now. Here is the best of over 25 years of rock guitar info from *Guitar Player,* selected to help you build a solid fretboard foundation, learn from the masters, and grab licks that you can use tonight. You've also got complete song transcriptions of three of the greatest rock guitar performances in history, by three of the most innovative and influential rock guitarists.

In another first from *Best Of Guitar Player* and Notes On Call, you can hear each lesson in this issue played by the best instructors in the business, on CD or audio cassette. Not only can you pick apart each lesson and lick by string, fret, and finger, but you can also hear exactly how it's supposed to sound. There's no better way to get to the heart of the music, and you just can't beat the price.

There's never been a rock 'n' roll collection like this. You'll learn the secrets and styles of the greats: Jimi Hendrix, Eric Clapton, Eddie Van Halen, Jeff Beck, Duane Allman, Eric Johnson, Ritchie Blackmore, Albert King, and Steve Cropper. Your instructors are the best, too: Joe Gore, Jesse Gress, Rik Emmett, Dave Rubin, and Jim Ferguson.

Don't wait another second. Dig in, and rock on.

—*Ernie Rideout*

Published by Miller Freeman Books
600 Harrison Street, San Francisco, CA 94107

E-mail: mfbooks@mfi.com
World Wide Web: http://www.books.mfi.com

Publishers of *Guitar Player, Bass Player* and *Keyboard* magazines

un Miller Freeman
A United News & Media publication

Distributed to the book trade in the U.S. and Canada by Publishers Group West, P.O. Box 8843, Emeryville, CA 94662

Distributed to the music trade in the U.S. and Canada by Hal Leonard Publishing, P.O. Box 13819, Milwaukee, WI 53213

ISBN 0-87930-403-0
Library of Congress No. 96-077863

Editor: Ernie Rideout
Cover Photo: Paul Haggard
Design: Samuel Miranda and Brad Greene

Printed in the United States of America
97 98 99 00 01   5 4 3 2 1

TABLE OF CONTENTS

NOTATION SYMBOLS

The following symbols are used in *Best of Guitar Player* to notate fingerings, techniques, and effects commonly used in guitar music. Certain symbols are found in either the tablature or the standard notation only, not both. For clarity, consult both systems.

4  : Left-hand fingering is designated by small Arabic numerals near note heads (1=first finger, 2=middle finger, 3=third finger, 4=little finger, t=thumb).

p  : Right-hand fingering designated by letters (p=thumb, i=first finger, m=middle finger, a=third finger, c=little finger).

②  : A circled number (1-6) indicates the string on which a note is to be played.

⊓ : Pick downstroke.

∨ : Pick upstroke.

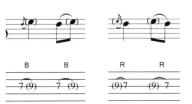

Bend: play the first note and bend to the pitch of the equivalent fret position shown in parentheses.

Reverse Bend: Pre-bend the note to the specified pitch/ fret position shown in parentheses. Play, then release to indicated pitch/fret.

Hammer-on: From lower to higher note(s). Individual notes may also be hammered.

Pull-off: From higher to lower note(s).

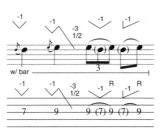

Slide: Play first note and slide up or down to the next pitch. If the notes are tied, pick only the first. If no tie is present, pick both.

A slide symbol before or after a single note indicates a slide to or from and undetermined pitch.

Finger vibrato.   Bar vibrato.

Bar dips, dives, and bends: Numerals and fractions indicate distance of bar bends in half-steps.

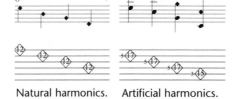

Natural harmonics.   Artificial harmonics.

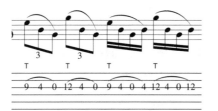

Pick-hand tapping: Notes are hammered with a pick-hand finger, usually followed by additional hammer-ons and pull-offs.

Trill.

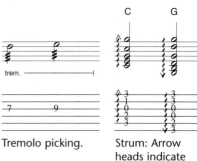

Tremolo picking.

Strum: Arrow heads indicate direction.

HOW TABLATURE WORKS

The horizontal lines represent the guitar's strings, the top line standing for the high *E.* The numbers designate the frets to be played. For instance, a 2 positioned on the first line would mean to play the 2nd fret on the first string (0 indicates an open string). Time values are indicated on the standard notation staff seen directly above the tablature. Special symbols and instructions appear between the standard and tablature staves.

CHORD DIAGRAMS

In all *Best of Guitar Player* chord diagrams, vertical lines represent the strings, and horizontal lines represent the frets. The following symbols are used:

━━━━━ Nut; indicates first position.

X   Muted string, or string not played.

O   Open string.

⌒   Barre (partial or full).

●   Placement of left-hand fingers.

III   Roman numerals indicate the fret at which a chord is located.

Arabic numerals indicate left-hand fingering.

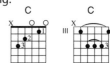

Eddie Van Halen:
My Tips for Beginners

BY JIM FERGUSON

Rock and roll is feeling. And after you know most of the basics — chords, scales, and bends, which I'll begin discussing in a minute — getting that feeling is just about the most important aspect of playing guitar.

In my opinion, you can't learn to play rock and roll by taking lessons. Although a teacher can show you certain things, such as songs and licks, you still have to sit down and learn how things feel by listening. My biggest influence was Eric Clapton when he was with Cream and John Mayall's Bluesbreakers. I learned his solos to "Crossroads" [from Cream's *Wheels Of Fire,* RSO] and "Sitting On Top of the World" [Cream, *Goodbye,* RSO] note-for-note by slowing them down to 16 RPM on my dad's turntable. By taking licks off records and listening, I developed a feel for rock and roll. If you want to play, that's the same kind of thing you'll have to do. Eventually, you'll take the phrases and rhythm patterns you've copped and begin to put your own mark on them.

One of the areas that guys put too much emphasis on is equipment. Once when Van Halen was on tour, we were opening for Ted Nugent and he was standing there watching me play, wondering how I did it. The next day at the soundcheck when I wasn't there, he asked our roadie if he could plug into my stuff. Of course, it still sounded like Ted. In other words, it doesn't really matter what you're playing through. Too many guys think a player's sound has to do with equipment, but it doesn't make any difference. Your sound is in your fingers and brain.

TRACK 1

If you're going to learn to play lead, get an electric guitar. It doesn't have to be an expensive one (I started on a cheapie Teisco Del Rey). Acoustic guitars aren't good for learning lead, because you can't play up very high on the neck, and they take heavier-gauge strings, which makes it hard to bend notes (I use light ones, Fender XLs). Also, you don't really need an amp at first, unless you're in a band. When I'm noodling around the house, I rarely plug in.

Most beginners want to learn lead because they think it's cool. Consequently, they never really develop good rhythm skills. Since most of a rock guitarist's time is spent playing rhythm, it's important to learn to do it well. Learning lead should come after you can play solid back-

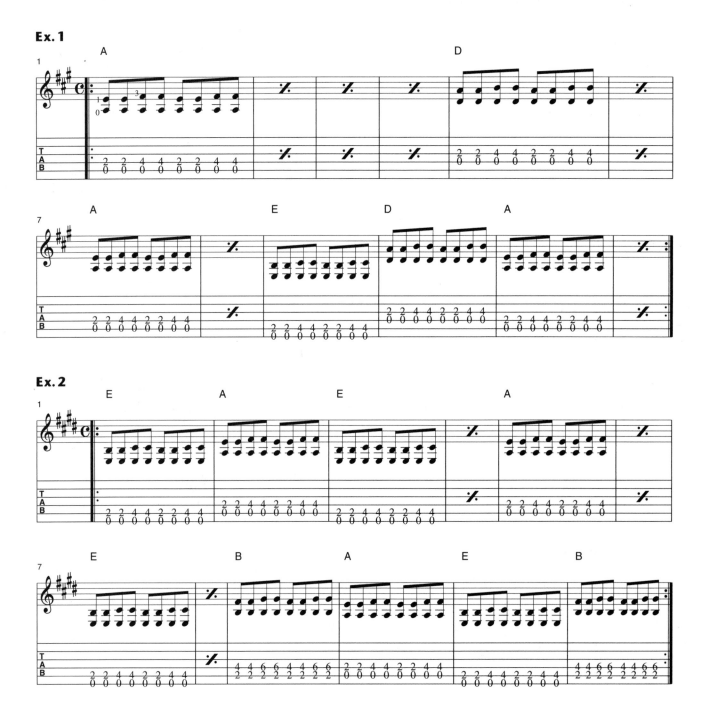

Ex. 1

Ex. 2

up and have the sound of the chords in your head.

Playing blues progressions is the best place to start learning, because they're so basic, and they form the foundation for a lot of rock tunes. After you get one or two patterns down in a couple of keys, you can start noodling with lead guitar. Ex.1 and Ex. 2 are two shuffle patterns in the keys of *A* and *E* respectively. Memorize them as soon as possible. Eventually, you'll want to learn them in some of the other common rock keys, such as *C*, *D*, and *G*. "Ice Cream Man," from our first album, and "Blues Breaker," which I did on Brian May's *Star Fleet Project,* are 12-bar blues.

I learned my first chords from a beginning guitar book that showed the usual *C, D, D7,* and *Em* down at the nut. But I rarely play chords like that. Listen to the difference between a regular *C* chord and this one, which sounds much more rock and roll:

Ex. 3

For a *G* chord I use this fingering (slightly muffle the bass notes with the heel of your right hand):

Ex. 4 G

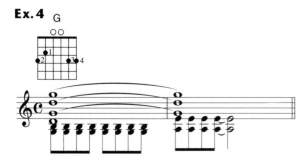

A lot of rock players mainly use barre chords, which employ the left-hand 1st finger to cover all six strings at a particular fret, but I usually just two-note it, like the beginning of "On Fire" from our LP *Van Halen*:

Ex. 5

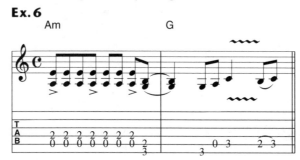

If you examine the first chord position in Ex.1, you'll see it's exactly the same as the two-note position we just looked at, except moved to the 12th fret and with no open strings.

Rhythm patterns can often be made more interesting by incorporating different riffs. The following example illustrates this. It's similar to what I do in "Ain't Talkin' 'Bout Love," also from *Van Halen*. It features a simple bass hook; try using all downstrokes for the two-note parts (more on right-hand picking in a moment):

Ex. 6

Later in "Ain't Talkin' 'Bout Love" I play the same chords in an arpeggio style. This is another good way to keep things from getting boring:

Ex. 7

Before we start working on playing lead, I want to talk about right-hand picking. Guys have pointed out that I hold my pick in two ways: with my thumb and middle finger (See Fig. 1), and with my thumb, index, and middle (see Fig. 2). Remember that most players don't pick the way I

Ex. 8

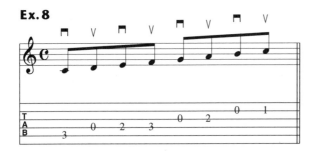

Fig. 1

Fig. 2

do, so what works for me might not work for you. The important thing about using the pick is that you alternate the picking direction: down, up, down, up, etc. (See Ex. 8.) This method really increases the efficiency of your picking hand. Once you get used to alternating strokes, you'll be able to pick without having to think about it.

The following position for the blues scale is the one most often used by blues and rock players. This scale fits many chords, including the *entire* 12-bar progression. If you already know this position, but still can't play lead very well, then you haven't worked with it enough (see Rik Emmet's Power of Five article on page 14). Once you learn some hammer-ons, pull-offs, slides, and bends, and how they're incorporated into licks, you'll see why the position is so common (be sure to use alternate picking):

Ex. 9

The next two patterns are the same as the one we just looked at, only in different locations. Knowing several patterns enables you to play over the entire length of the fingerboard. Also, different positions lend themselves to different licks.

Ex. 10

Ex. 11

Another common scale position is the following long form, which spans from the 3rd to the 12th fret. Note that when it descends, the notes are played on different strings; however, you can go backwards through the ascending pattern (if you do, use your 1st finger to shift downward). Notice that when you go up, the 3rd finger is used to get to each new position. Also, the area around the 7th fret can produce some especially nice phrases.

Ex. 12

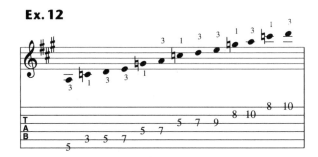

Ex. 13   **Ex. 14**

Ex. 15   **Ex. 16**

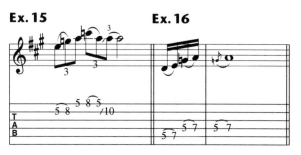

Once you have these scale patterns memorized, it's time to learn how to move them to other keys. For instance, the first pattern becomes an *E* scale when moved to the 12th fret. You can easily figure this out by moving the root of the scale up the fingerboard chromatically (the root is the note that has the same name as the scale). For example, on the sixth string the note at the 5th fret is an *A*; at the 6th fret it's an *A#* (or a *Bb* — they're the same); at the 7th fret it's a *B*, and so on until you get to the 12th fret. Here's the complete chromatic scale so you can move other patterns on your own (once you get to the end of the scale, *G#*, continue ascending by starting over at *A*). As long as you know the name of the scale or chord you're starting with, you can move up or down through the chromatic scale; each letter represents one fret (don't use open strings).

A   A#(Bb)   B   C   C#(Db)   D   D#(Eb)   E   F   F#(Gb)   G   G#(Ab)

But knowing note locations is just the beginning. The next step is to start learning the building blocks of licks: hammer-ons, pull-offs, bends, and slides. Hammer-ons and pull-offs can give the notes you play fluidity and speed. The following phrases are a few short examples for the scale position at the 5th fret. From here it's your responsibility to transfer the techniques to other phrases and positions:

Bending is probably the technique most often associated with blues and rock soloing, and for that reason it's the most important one to learn. If you're a beginner, there are a couple of things to watch out for. First, don't overshoot the bend. By that I mean don't bend a note beyond where you intend to go. And once a note is bent, be careful not to use too much finger vibrato — a singing effect produced by rapidly wiggling a string with a finger of your left hand right after it's been played. If your vibrato wavers too much, you'll overshoot the bend and it'll sound weird.

Here's an exercise for developing bending accuracy. If you can bend with the left-hand pinky, fine; but most players use the 3rd finger because it's stronger. The other fingers can support the one doing the bending. Most bends in rock and blues go up one whole-step; get the correct note in your head by playing the *A* on the second string, 10th fret. Practice bending right up to the *A*. If you hold the note for a while, use slight vibrato:

Ex. 17

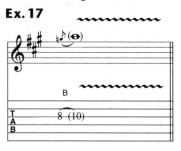

Now let's learn the bend in combination with some other notes. (A bend *starts* with a bent note, and then releases it.)

Ex. 18 **Ex. 19**

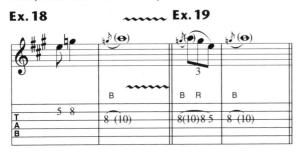

Ex. 20 **Ex. 21**

Lots of guys ask which notes I like to bend the most, and I always say all of them. And that's true, depending on the song I'm playing. However, some notes are bent more than others. The example we just looked at uses one of the most commonly bent notes. Remember its position in relation to the scale pattern at the 5th fret — it's on the second string and played with the third finger — so you can use it in other keys. Two other good notes to bend, also played with the 3rd finger, are located on the third string, 7th fret (*D*, see Fig. 3) and first string, 8th fret (*C*). Here are some licks using both notes, combining them with hammers, pulls, and slides. Practice them until they become second nature; then find their location in the other scale patterns. Once things feel comfortable, work on playing lead in different keys and with a variety of rhythms.

Fig. 3

Sometimes I think of a new technique or lick at the strangest times. When I got the idea for right-hand tapping, I was in the bathroom with my

Ex. 22 **Ex. 23**

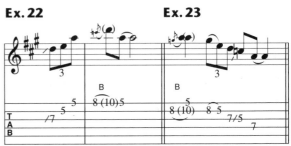

guitar. This technique is often written incorrectly in books and played wrong, so here's how it works. To understand the idea (behind right-hand tapping), first play this trill with your left hand:

Ex. 24

Now tap a finger of your right hand — I usually use the 1st or 2nd — to produce the first note, and then pull it off of the string to sound the second (see Fig. 4). The pull-off motion should be toward you, and should slightly catch the string. Whole descending scales can be

Fig. 4

played in this way; try it with the first blues pattern we discussed.

Ex. 25

Once you understand the basic moves of tapping (sounding the note with your right hand and pulling off), then you're ready to apply it to a lick. Here's a thing I do in the last part of "Eruption," from *Van Halen* (it can also be played on the third string). It's really easy, and makes a great exercise. Notice that after you tap and pull off, you then hammer down to get the third note. Experiment enough with this technique and you'll realize you can get many other combinations.

Ex. 26

Ex. 27

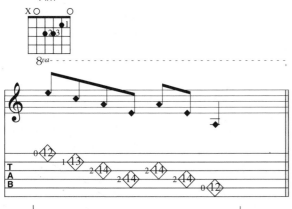

tap 12 frets above fret hand positions

Another easy right-hand technique is harmonic tapping. Examples of this can be heard on "Spanish Fly," "Women In Love" [both from *Van Halen II*] "Eruption," and "Top Jimmy" [*1984*]. In order to produce a harmonic, just tap 12 frets above a note, directly on the fret (remove your right-hand finger quickly). Although you can do this technique on an acoustic instrument, you'll get better results on an electric (see Fig. 5 and Ex. 27).

Now that you know some of the basic ingredients of rock and roll, remember that your playing has to have feeling and taste. The goal is to make music, not always to play machine gun-type stuff. To me, music is entertainment. You shouldn't be playing it to save the world or show people how great you are. It's just supposed to make you happy, make you cry, or whatever. If it doesn't do that, then it's not music. And remember: You learn by making mistakes. Don't be afraid to try something new. If I'm thrown into an unfamiliar situation, such as playing with Allan Holdsworth, I don't panic. Sometimes I skin my knees, but most of the time I land on my feet. My dad has a Dutch saying that puts it much better than I can: Translated, it means, "Ride your bicycle straight through." If you screw up, just keep going.

Fig. 5

The Power of Five
Getting a Grip on Pentatonics

BY RIK EMMETT

verybody has music that's a landmark in the soundtrack of their lives. One of mine is Led Zeppelin's debut album *(Led Zeppelin,* Atlantic]. When I recently rediscovered it on CD, it conjured up powerful memories of 1969, when I was a 16-year-old basement-band guitarist. There I was, in my boyhood bedroom, my trusty one-pickup Kay in hand. I was wearing out the needle on the old Seabreeze, trying to decipher the beautiful, cascading run that Jimmy Page plays on "Communication Breakdown," when the proverbial light-bulb went on over my head. "Hey, that cool pattern he plays over *E* major is the same one I'd use if I were playing blues in the key of C#! I had discovered the beautiful duplicity of the pentatonic scale. If I went three frets below wherever I was playing the basic blues scale pattern, the same fingering yielded a majorish "country" sound.

A pentatonic scale (from the Greek penta, meaning five) has five notes in each octave. The folk music of many cultures is on pentatonic scales. ("Auld Lang Syne," for example, has a pentatonic melody.) We usually encounter pentatonic scales in one of two contexts: as a *major pentatonic scale,* with root, 2, 3, 5, and 6 (you can think of it as a major scale that's "missing" scale degrees 4 and 7 — see Ex. 1); or as a *minor pentatonic* or *blues* scale, with root ♭3, 4, 5, and ♭7 (see Ex. 2 — the ♭3 and ♭7 of the blues pentatonic scale are the legendary "blue notes").

TRACK 2

Ex. 1

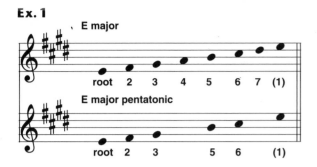

Ex. 2

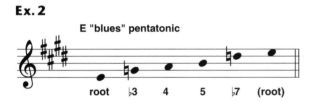

Ex. 3

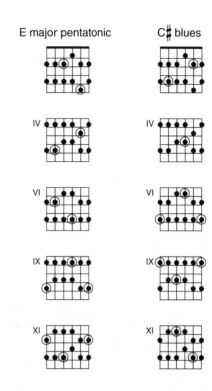

Here's Rik Emmett's party trick #278: Drag your fingers harp-style across a piano's black keys while holding down the sustain pedal. Not only will everyone be impressed by the guitarist who has been so modestly concealing his keyboard chops, but you'll have played a G♭ major pentatonic scale (or an E♭ blues scale — remember E♭ is three frets below G♭).

Each pentatonic fingering can be interpreted as either major or blues/minor, depending on which note you designate as the root. Ex. 3 shows major and minor pentatonic scale fingerings (for E major and C# blues, respectively) in five positions. Notice that the fingerings are the same for both scale types, but that different notes serve as the root.

The two pentatonic scales are not mutually exclusive. Our culture's pop music has assimilated both, so you can combine them in the same song, solo, or heck even in the same bar of a riff. Try playing over a 12-bar blues progression using the blues/minor pentatonic fingerings Then, try sliding any of the five fingerings down three frets to get the major "country" sound. Getting a grasp of this concept is a good first step towards understanding the more advanced modal superimposition concepts of players such as Frank Gambale and Larry Carlton.

A word about the power of the number five: The fifth is the most basic, powerful interval, the

Circle of Fifths is a fundamental concept in music theory, and the ancient Chinese revered the number five because it signified the five elements, the five types of human relationships, and the five types of grain. In our microtonal, polychromatic world, the pentatonic scale is a profound, primal means of expression that we still may not appreciate or understand fully enough.

The Five Block System. Let's examine one of the most important concepts for understanding the fingerboard: the block system. In the Jan. '87 *Guitar Player* 20th Anniversary issue, Jim Ferguson wrote a retrospective feature on "Classic Columns." Humility may have caused him to overlook his own very deserving "Scale Systems" feature from July '84, an article I've recommend often. That column introduces readers to the classic five-block system, which is based on five simple first position chord forms (Ex. 4).

Ex. 4

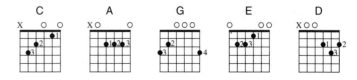

Ex. 5

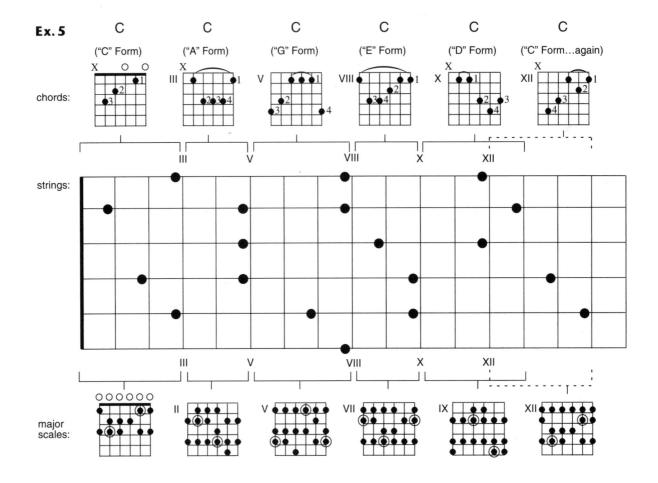

Now let's take the five forms and put them on the fingerboard as different voicings of the same chord, in the same key, all the way up the neck (Ex. 5). Don't get confused — the chords at the top of Ex. 5 are all C chords, but they're labeled according to the visual shape of the first position chords. The diatonic major scales that correspond to each chord form are shown at the bottom of the example. The root notes — all C's in this case — are circled. It's not the pin-up foldout of the month, but you may want to photocopy Ex. 5 and tack it up in your practice area. It's prob-ably the most important building block of fret-board knowledge.

Now you've got a system that covers the entire fingerboard. Your challenge is to transpose it into all the major keys. After 30,000 fretboard miles, you should be able to do it *stone cold*.

The Five W's. Once you've figured out the five-block major scale patterns in all keys, you can double-check your work against Ex. 6 and Ex. 7. Those of you who claim that the dog ate your homework should feel ashamed — consider these offerings a free introductory gift. Come up with

Ex. 6   G scale system

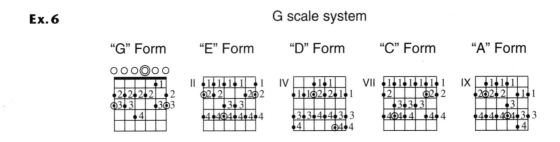

Ex. 7

E scale system

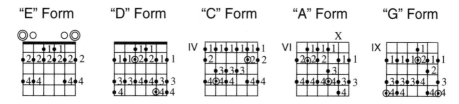

"E" Form   "D" Form   "C" Form   "A" Form   "G" Form

fingerings for the other nine keys on your own, and say three "Hail Chuck Berrys" as penance for your indolence.

To fully assimilate the five-block system into your playing, you must connect the dots. How will you shift from one scale position to the next? Ex. 8 shows one way to combine three positions in order to execute a smooth run. In the ascending run, the first five notes come from the "*E*-form" *G* scale. The arrow represents a shift up to the "*D*-form" *G* scale for the next seven notes. A second shift takes you up to the "*C*-form" *G* scale for the final six notes.

When and where to shift is a matter of personal choice — comfort and ease of memorization are the most important criteria. (Attention dog-feeders: This doesn't mean that you don't have to work it out!)

Ex. 8

Ascending G major scale   Descending G major scale

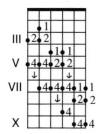 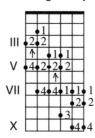

Before signing off on the topic of five, here's one more thing to chew on: Journalists are taught to address the five W's: who, what, when, where, and why. Musicians should ask themselves the same questions.

Who? Have I committed my heart and soul to the music? Who is my audience, and *am* I reaching them?

What? Do I understand what I'm doing? Do I have perspective and awareness? What is the significance of the music to me and my audience?

When? Timing is everything. Is my playing appropriate? Am I playing the right note at the right time? Am I adding to the groove? Can I give the performance a real sense of occasion?

Where? "Where" is closely related to "when." I once saw Larry Carton and B.B. King together on a TV show. Larry said that when he wanted to improve his phrasing and placement, he went back to B.B.'s records and found that he was playing everywhere that B.B. wasn't and vice versa. He turned his playing around, and the rest is history.

Finally, **Why?** A good actor searches for motivation. If you want to make it really matter, you've got to have a reason. You don't necessarily have to spell it out for your audience, but if you know why you're playing something, they'll know the difference.

Pull Out The Stops
Increase Your Chord Vocabulary With Double and Triple Stops

BY DAVE RUBIN

ouble Stops. Like Little Richard, who once proclaimed himself both the king and queen of rock and roll, double-stops have dual distinctions: They can function as chordal indicators, harmonized solos, or both.

Double-stops are classified according to the interval between the low and high note. Let's check out double-stops in sixths. (Thirds, fourths, and fifths are other common intervals found in most forms of music.) In pop music, most double-stops are derived from the Ionian (major), Aeolian (natural minor), and Mixolydian (dominant) modes. Ex. 1 harmonizes the *G* Mixolydian mode (1, 2, 3, 4, 5, 6, ♭7 = *G, A, B, C, D, E, F*) on the first and third strings; Ex. 2 transfers the same idea to the second and fourth strings. I've notated the scales horizontally over the span of an octave, though they can also be played in a single position across shifting pairs of strings.

Ex. 3 contains the classic "sliding 9th" lick found in blues standards like "Stormy Monday." It's constructed from the *G* and *C* Mixolydian modes (bars 1 and 2, respectively). This is totally cool as a lead/rhythm part against a guitar or keyboard banging out triplet chords over a slow 12/8 groove.

Chuck Berry's "Memphis" is based on the sliding pattern in Ex. 4. The effect is that of a major chord (suggested by scale degrees 1 and 3, *G* and *B*) shifting to a dominant chord (♭7 and 9, *F* and *A*). For a real greasy I-IV-V progression, shift the lick to the IV and V chords (*C* at the 8th fret and *D* at the 10th fret).

TRACK 3

Ex. 1

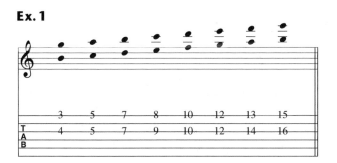

Ex. 2

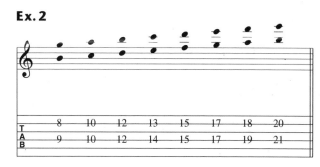

Ex. 3

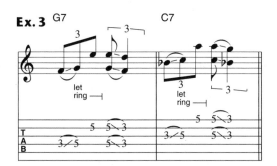

Ex. 4

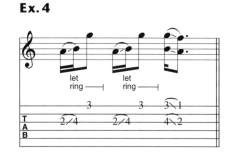

Ex. 5

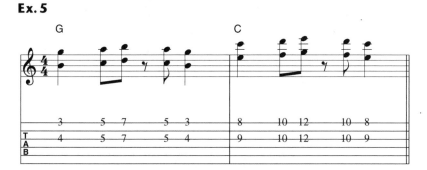

Ex. 6

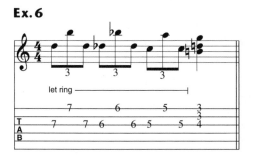

Ex. 5 uses some garden-variety doublestops found in the intro hook of Van Morrison's "Brown-Eyed Girl." The second bar implies the IV chord (C) and can be seen as the first three degrees of a harmonized C Mixolydian mode, or as the 4th, 5th, and 6th degrees of G Mixolydian. As you can see, the Mixolydian mode is a helpful tool for covering I-IV changes. Robert Johnson's signature dominant/diminished chord turnaround can be reduced to the double-stop sequence in Ex. 6. Note that a passing interval

($B\flat$/$D\flat$) has been inserted between the 2nd and 3rd degrees of the G Mixolydian mode. This implied diminished chord ensures a smooth transition to the root triad.

Theoretically speaking, chords need at least three notes to be fully defined. But we can substitute double-stops for chords if we carefully match the key signatures. Remember, when you are conscious of the proper changes, you will always be harmonically — if not politically — correct.

Triple Stops. Three-note chord forms were extensively employed by rock guitarists even before '60s British bands like the Kinks began overdriving their AC30s. Amid the current disarray of grunge, punk-funk, and pop bands, it seems prudent for the thinking guitarist to rise above the morass by expanding his or her chordal vocabulary with triple-stops, which are groups of three simultaneous notes.

Triple-stops are often triads. The most common triads are major (1, 3, 5), minor (1, ♭3, 5), augmented (1, 3, #5), and diminished (1, ♭3, ♭5). Dominant chords — 7ths, 9ths, 13ths, and the like — theoretically require at least four notes, but they can often be implied with triple-stops. While Ex. 10 lacks the root *A*, it can function as *A7*, especially if another instrument supplies the missing tonic.

Ex. 1 displays the *A* major scale harmonized in triads. Memorize these useful forms in all the major keys. The diagonal lines in the chord names indicate that these are inversions; their lowest

Ex. 1

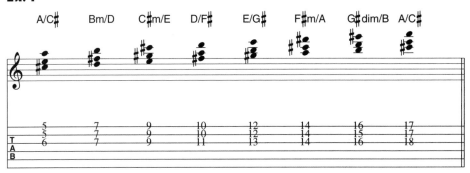

Ex. 2

Ex. 3

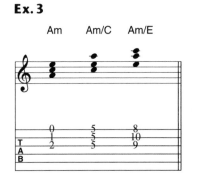

Ex. 4

Ex. 5

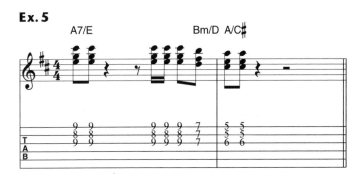

Ex. 6

notes are not their roots. Such inversions are sometimes called "slash chords" (no, not that Slash, thank you). Please note that the seventh chord in the series, G#m♭5, has the same shape as Ex. 4's rootless dominant 7 chord. Context is all-important when identifying three-note chords.

Ex. 2 shows the root position and first and second inversions of an A major triad. This series sounds slick as a substitute for a single chord. Ex. 3 shows the corresponding A minor and inversions. If you go back to Ex. 1 and work out the root positions and inversions for each triad, you'll probably get a headache. You will also have enough chord forms ready to express yourself with more vim and verve.

Lots of classic blues and rock tunes feature three-note chords. Ex. 5 is based on a theme that appears in "Killing Floor." "I Fought The Law" and "Peggy Sue" both use patterns similar to Ex. 6. Ex. 7 shows how triadic inversions can help connect a chord progression. Notice how the melody note on the high-E string descends chromatically from A to E — hip stuff! Both "Hotel California" and "Wild Horses" can be arranged in this manner.

Ex. 7

Finding Your Roots

BY DAVE RUBIN

lbert King's classic "Born Under A Bad Sign" was released as a single in '67 and was the title tune of King's landmark '68 album. A generation of English and American blues guitarists, from Eric Clapton to Stevie Ray Vaughan, fell under the spell of Albert's time-warp string bending and dramatic phrasing.

"Born Under A Bad Sign" does not follow the conventional 12-bar, I-IV-V arrangement, it contains verses of eight and ten bars. The main vocal verses are 12 measures long, however, with the I chord maintained for eight bars before changing to the V, IV, and I. This extended I chord creates a hypnotic tension that's reinforced by the unison guitar/bass line and Albert's stabbing lead fills. In order to give a sense of the entire song, I have combined a four-bar intro with the 12-bar verse. I have also harmonized the bass line in double-stops; everyone from Chuck Berry to Jimi Hendrix has used this simple but effective device to add body and soul to basic pentatonic scales. Also note that I have transposed the tune from the original key of D♭ to the more blues-friendly key of G.

The early '60s were a grim period in American popular culture — moronic TV sitcoms, button-down madras shirts, and white-bread "hootenanny" music. Rock was reeling, what with Buddy dead, Chuck in stir, and Jerry Lee banished. Some of the only hot wax around was instrumental rock, much of it blues-based and guitar powered.

TRACK 5/6

Booker T. & the MGs, anchored by guitarist Steve Cropper and bassist Donald "Duck" Dunn, were the premier R&B instrumental group of the era. In 1961, however, they were part of an organ combo called the Mar-Keys when they released "Last Night." The organ/guitar tandem on this classic tune helped establish the framework for Booker T.'s 1962 smash "Green Onions" and the great Memphis soul music that followed.

This arrangement of the tune's head combines parts of the horn section, organ, and guitar licks. As with most ensemble music that's

Born Under A Bad Sign
By William Bell and Booker T. Jones

been distilled down to solo guitar, some editing was necessary. In this case, it is the organ represented by the *B♭* and *B* notes over the I chord and the *E♭* and *E* over the IV. But when the entire piece is phrased properly and precisely, you'll get a dynamic harmony worthy of the original.

Listening to the original "Last Night" will aid your learning process. Also, on the CD, you can hear me play the arrangements as written, along with additional ideas.

Last Night
By Charles Axton, Gilbert Caple, Chips Maman, Floyd Newman, and Jerry Smith

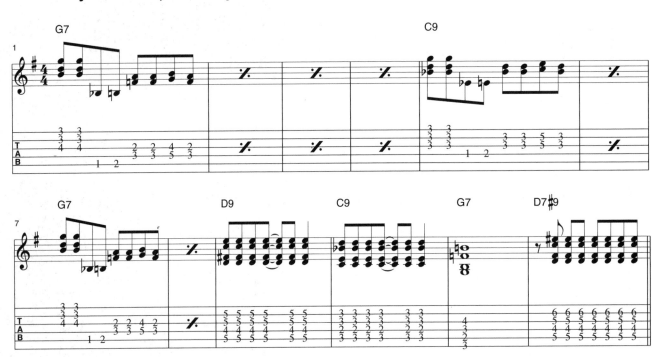

LAST NIGHT, by Lloyd Newman, Gilbert Caple, Charles Axton, Jerry Smith and Chips Moman
© 1961 (Renewed) Irving Music, Inc. (BMI) All Rights Reserved Used by Permission
WARNER BROS. PUBLICATIONS U.S. INC., Miami, FL 33014

The Complete Song Transcription!
"Savoy"
By Jeff Beck

TEXT BY JESSE GRESS

Jeff Beck's magical fingerstyle is so well-integrated with his whammy bar wizardry that listeners and transcribers alike have been fooled into thinking they were hearing slide guitar. At times, Beck's subtle bar-bouncing might even be mistaken for a whacked-out harmonica or saxophone, not to mention an alumnus of the Bulgarian women's choir! When the master mechanic emerged with *Guitar Shop* [Epic] in 1989, he finessed like never before.

The intro to "Savoy" is pure, ravaging Beck while the head beginning at A hints at a pre-"Crazy Legs" tribute to Cliff Gallup. The muscular triple-stop bends could be simulated by pulling up on a floating whammy bar, but to sound like the master, you're gonna have to bend 'em for real! Jeff's faux-slide shows up in the C and F sections along with several signature adjacent string and bar-bent trills. Grace bends or whammy bar dips are notated with bar notation only, while rhythmic bar bends are fully notated.

The 6th-string harmonic rave-up at G may be played between the 2nd and 4th frets, but Beck used his fret-hand to reach over and bounce the bar while his right hand played Jaco-style harmonics (à la "Birdland") off the fingerboard. See the footnote in the score for details. The pseudo-crowd noises harken back to "Blues Deluxe" from Jeff's first album, *Truth* [Epic].

The double-time solo drips with the kind of edge-of-the-seat thrills 'n' chills that personify Beck at his best. Like the intro, the faster passages are alternate-picked using the index-finger and nail supported by the thumb, as if you were holding a pick. Returning post-solo to the half-time feel, Beck weaves a series of majestic high-register melodies, including a tip-of-the-Strat to Moogmeister Jan Hammer in bars 147-150 that brings things to a crashing close. Whew!

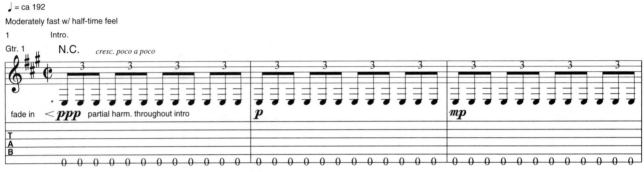

* Played with thumb and index finger pinched together as if holding a pick.

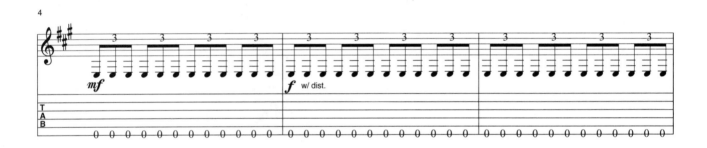

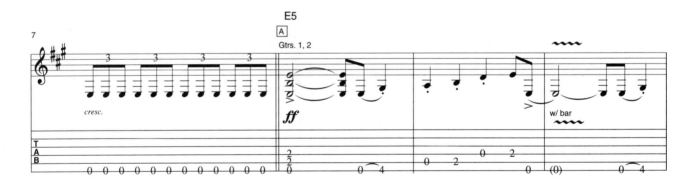

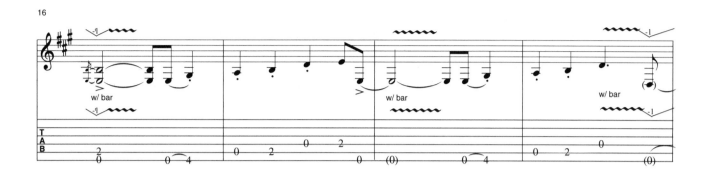

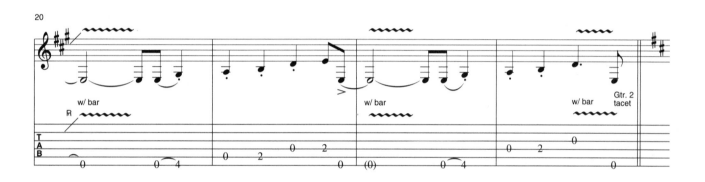

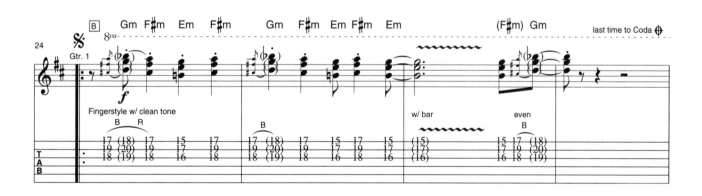

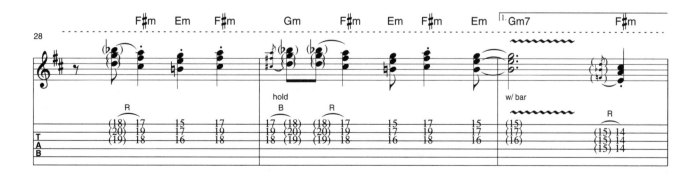

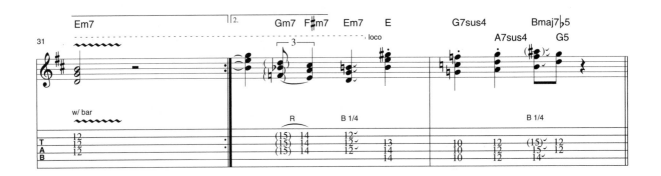

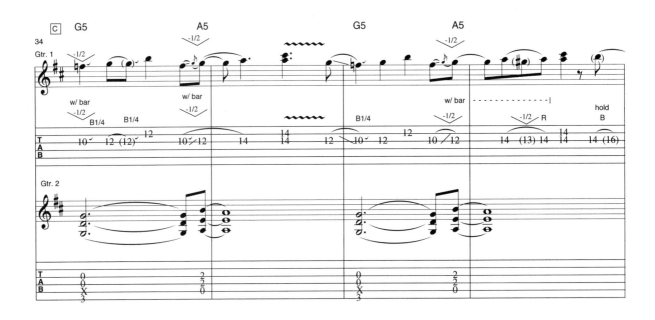

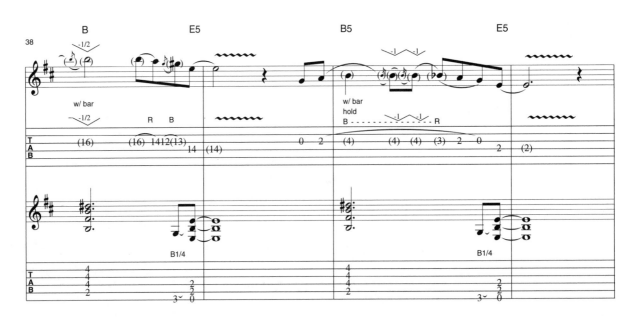

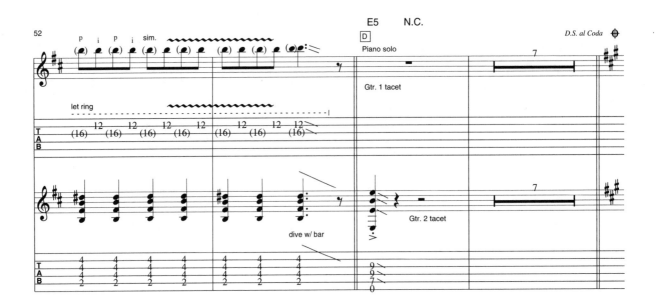

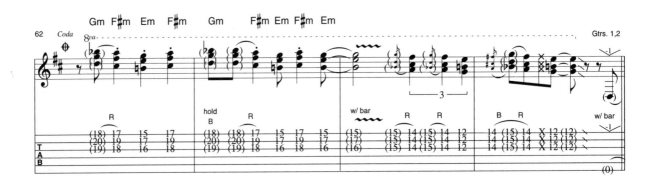

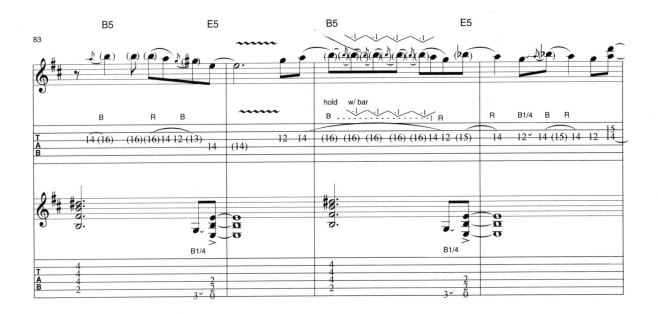

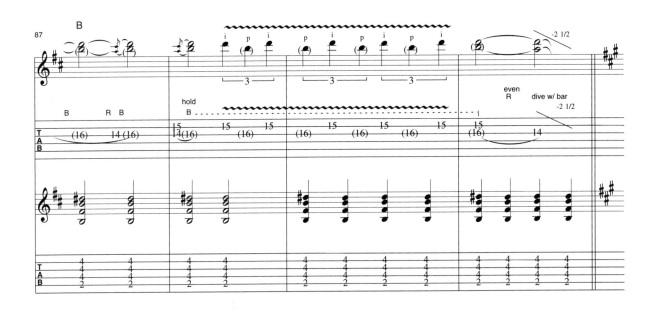

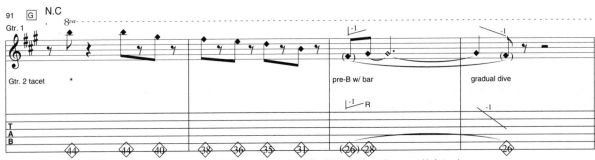

* Harmonics are played at approximate, theoretical fret positions off fingerboard, "Jaco-style." The right thumb is used as a movable fret and positioned over the node while the string is plucked behind it using the index or ring finger. The left hand "bounces" the vibrato bar as written.

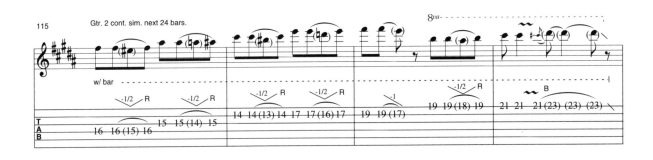

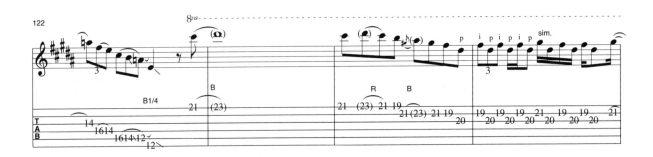

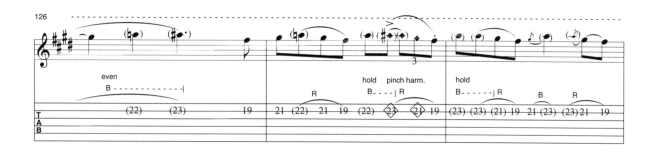

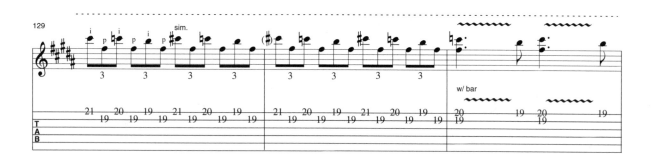

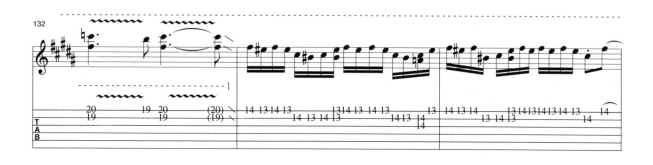

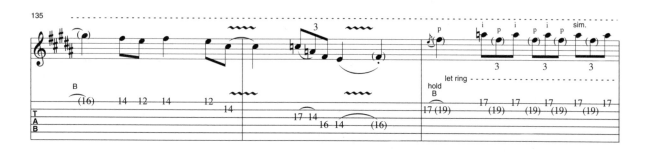

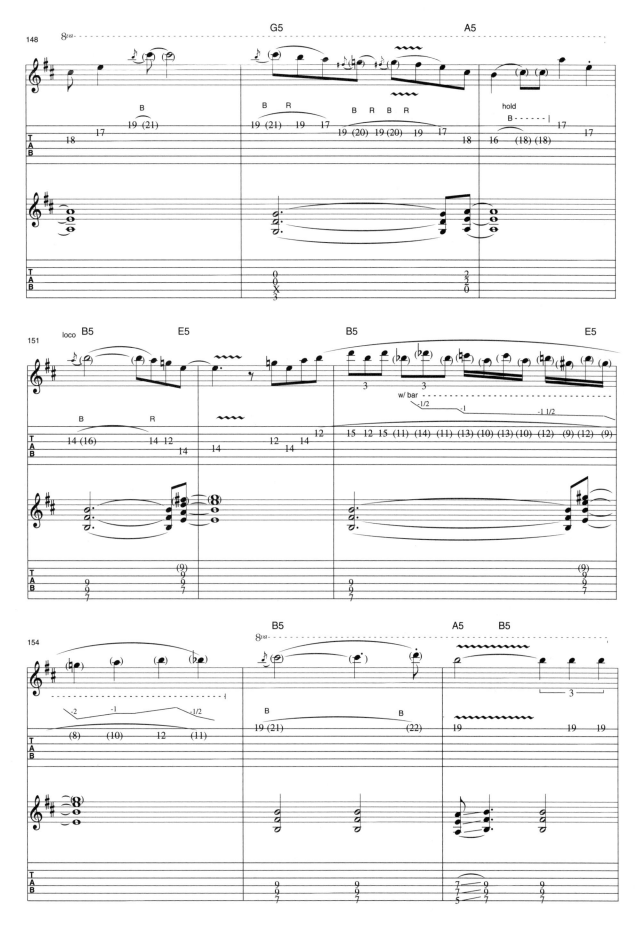

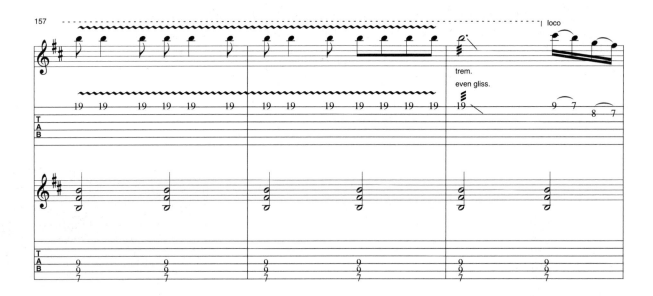

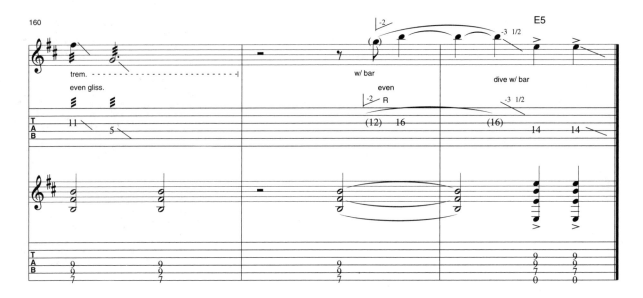

SAVOY, by Jeff Beck, Terry Bozzio and Tony Hymas

© 1989 WB Music COrp. & BHB Music Limited All Rights o/b/o BHB Music Limited for the World, excluding Japan, administered by WB Music Corp. All Rights Reserved
Used by Permission WARNER BROS. PUBLICATIONS U.S. INC., Miami, FL 33014

Hendrix and Rhythm
The Most Essential Thing

BY RIK EMMETT

Everyone pays lip service to the Hendrix legacy, but the hyperbole, apocrypha, and exploitation that have shrouded Jimi's artistic accomplishments may have discouraged some younger guitarists from exploring his contributions in depth. There's a lot more there than attention-getting dental work, behind-the-back passes, and lighter-fluid pyrotechnics. Let's focus on just one of Hendrix's many talents: rhythm playing.

"This is a world of lead guitar players, but the most essential thing to learn is the time, the rhythm." —Jimi Hendrix

"That's why he liked rhythm playing so much — the rhythm guitar could lay out the structure for the whole song." —Mike Bloomfield

There's the whole lesson neatly wrapped up in two quotes. Lead guitar playing starts out as a world of riffs, scales, and patterns. Would-be lead players often become obsessed with fancy techniques, dedicating all their energy to just a fraction of the total picture. Chances are, your favorite solo is just a small part of a larger musical structure of verses, choruses, and so forth, an architecture composed of three basic ingredients: *melody, harmony,* and *rhythm.*

A solo performs a *melodic* function (and possibly a secondary harmonic or rhythmic one if the solo section itself stands in contrast to the rest of the song). But a great rhythm guitar part performs integral harmonic and rhythmic functions. Too many Fancy Dan guitarists ignore this all-important two-thirds. But Jimi, one of the greatest Fancy Dans ever to touch down on this third stone from the sun, knew

TRACK 7

what the word "rhythm" meant in rhythm and blues, and understood that "rock and roll" referred to musical interpretations of body movement.

Rhythm guitar playing is not an egotistical pursuit. It's a marriage to the structure, a complete union with the piece of music. Rhythm playing sublimates itself to serve the *whole picture.* If the soloist can be described as someone who searches for self-expression by riding the vehicle of the song, then the rhythm player can be seen as the perfect cog — or the lubricating oil, or even the ghost — in the machine.

Some of Jimi's finest moments occur in his R&B-style ballads such as "Little Wing," "The Wind Cries Mary," and "Angel." Ex. 1 tries to cap-

ture that style, with little chord fills ornamented with major-pentatonic noodling. Note how the 2nd scale degree hammers into the 3rd, often in the bottom voice of a chord. Play it with a laid-back, loosey-goosey feel, almost letting the grace notes become sixteenth-notes. If you normally use a hard pick, try a softer one.

Let's look at some of the techniques that appear in "All Along The Watchtower," perhaps Jimi's best-known solo. The song's second solo is divided into four eight-bar sections. Jimi starts with a "regular" lead guitar sound, moves on to 12-string slide with heavy echo and compression, follows with wah-wah with echo, and finally — you guessed it — a *rhythm solo!*

Ex. 1

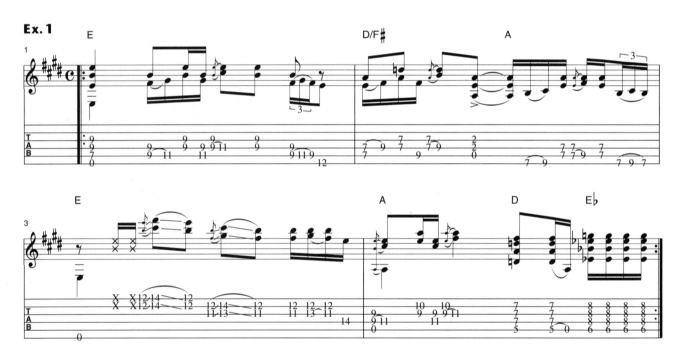

Ex. 2 (see next page) is an exercise along those lines. Again, we find a number of chords with the 9th on top, while many chords are only suggested by two-string, Chuck Berry-type figures that omit the 3rd. Try playing bars 3 and 4 with the same aggressive, all-downstroke approach that Jimi uses at the end of the "Watchtower" solo. The idea isn't to display awesome technique, but to physically move you because it grooves so well. That's the quality all great rhythm playing has, be it Freddie Green, Keith Richards, Melissa Etheridge, Phil Upchurch, or Jimi; let's call it *propulsion.*

Want to hear what I mean? Listen to what Jimi does after the band kicks into the groove of "Purple Haze" — he propels the music forward with his rhythm work. There are thousands of other examples I could cite of Jimi's recordings to illustrate the value of propulsion over flash, but space limitations force me to suggest that you just get your hands on Jimi's first four albums and try to get into the musical Experience.

Also, you might study Ex. 3. Set your metronome to a slow tempo, about 60 beats per minute, and then get your strumming hand brushing up and down across the strings in a sixteenth-note groove. Start by accenting on the beat (ONE-ee-and-uh, TWO-ee-and-uh, THREE-ee-and-uh, FOUR ee-and-uh). After you have that solid as a rock, you're ready to try for the first hallmark of great rhythm playing: putting em-PHA-sis in in-ter-EST-ing places.

Ex. 2

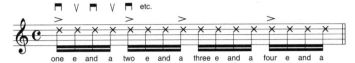

Ex. 3

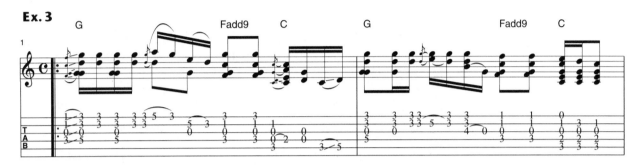

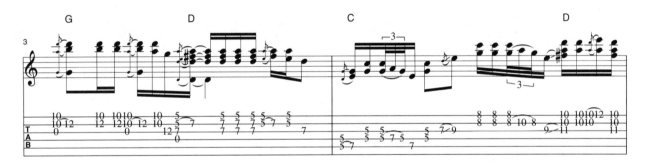

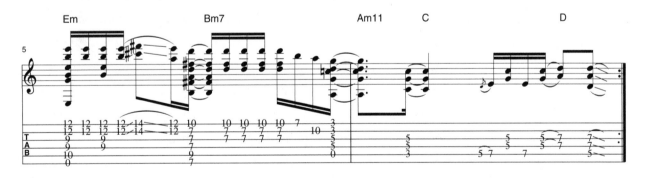

Ex. 1 is an excerpt from ALL ALONG THE WATCHTOWER by Bob Dylan
Copyright © 1968, 1985 Dwarf Music, International Copyright Secured. All Rights Reserved.
Reprinted by Permission of Music Sales Corporation (ASCAP).

Wah-Wah User's Guide
A Lesson from the Masters

BY JOE GORE

Nothing reveals inexperienced wah wankers so readily as their tendency to simply rock the pedal on the beat. No shame in that — most of us have a hard enough time playing without bringing a third limb into the equation. Tapping a foot in time to the music is probably the safest way to begin.

But of course, the true wizards of wah approach the pedal much less predictably. They sculpt each note to best suit the musical context, which requires a level of hand/foot coordination that may seem elusive at first. Consider the famous riff from the Jimi Hendrix *Electric Ladyland* classic "Voodoo Chile (Slight Return)": Ex.1 shows the passage that commences about 10 seconds into the song. The wah notation — "O" for "open" (maximum treble) position and, later in this lesson, a circled "X" for "closed" (minimum treble) position — is admittedly crude. It doesn't take into account the spectrum of sounds available between the two extreme settings. But even so, we can see how free and funky Jimi's accents are.

Since the "open" position is the wah's loudest sound, notes played in that way stand out in relation to their neighbors (*duh!* — but bear with me). In the first four bars, the wah accents tend to fall on the offbeat eighth-notes (the "and" of each beat), implying a subtle double-time backbeat feel, almost as if snare hits were occurring there. The drums enter at the end of bar 4, at which point Jimi turns the feel around, placing most of the accents on the downbeats along with Mitch Mitchell's bass drum. Too tough.

TRACK 8

How can one cultivate this sort of rhythmic unpredictability, the independence of motion that lets our hands and feet perform different tasks simultaneously? Let's take a clue from drummers, who often devote huge amounts of energy to cultivating the kinetic independence of each limb. C'mon — if *drummers* can do it, you certainly can.

Ex. 1

Declaration of Independence. Ex. 2a is probably the next easiest thing to tapping the wah on the beat. Offbeat wah rhythms are most readily playable when the foot motion doubles a corresponding hand motion. Here the wah is depressed into open/treble position for the highest notes of the riff. (The crescendo/decrescendo wedges indicate the opening and closing of the pedal.) Again, we're implying a snare-like backbeat feet. After you can play Ex. 2a comfortably with a metronome at a medium rock tempo — 120 bpm, say — try Ex. 2b. It's the same wah pattern, but set against a single note. Your foot is no longer cued by the motion of your hands.

Ex. 2a

Ex. 2b

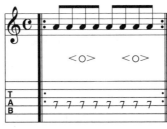

Ex. 2c

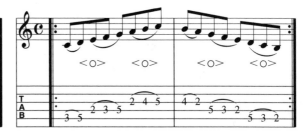

Next, try maintaining the wah pattern against a melodic figure that doesn't correspond to the foot pattern — a major or pentatonic scale, for example. As you become more confident, try patterns like Ex. 2c, in which the hand motions — pick strokes, melodic contour, placement of string changes and slurs — occur completely independently of the wah accents.

Examples 3a through 3g are other rhythmic patterns that you can subject to the same three-step process we used in Ex. 2. Try each figure first using a high note to mark the wah accent, as notated; next, try it on just a single note; finally, try superimposing the wah pattern over different melodies. Change the notes (those octave E's get old real fast) or work with double-stops and full chords. Contrast clean, clearly articulated notes with percussive scratching. And after you can play these at about 140 bpm or more, halve the tempo and try the examples as sixteenth-note funk feels.

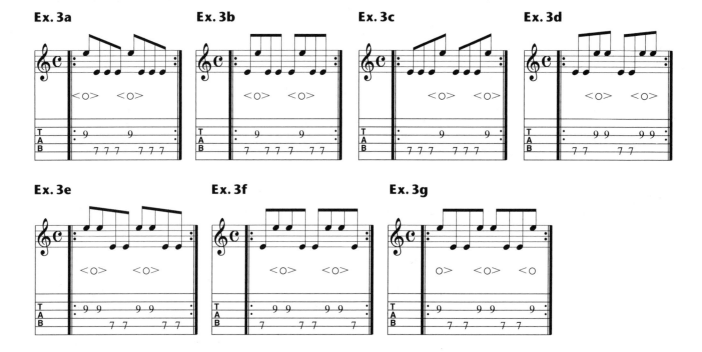

Ex. 3a **Ex. 3b** **Ex. 3c** **Ex. 3d**

Ex. 3e **Ex. 3f** **Ex. 3g**

Sweeps, flutters, yuks, and gulps. So far, our examples have focused on fast opening and closing of the wah filter. But long sweeps are equally cool. A gradual opening and closing can flavor an extended solo — just ask Kirk Hammett — or impart a funky, analog synth-like filter envelope to a short, repetitious figure. Ex. 4 evokes an early '70s wah style exemplified by the guitar part on Isaac Hayes' "Theme From *Shaft.*" The wah opens slowly, but there is a clear dynamic accent on the fourth beat of each measure. "Tracking" the melodic contour of a long line (Ex. 5) is also effective.

Ex. 4

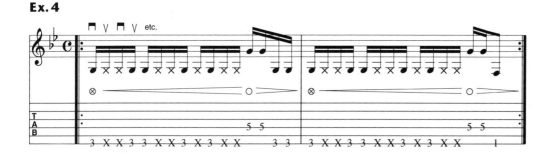

Ex. 5

Another trippy sound is a rapid flutter, most effective against sustained chords. Eric Clapton uses this device to good effect on the bridge of Cream's "White Room" (from *Wheels of Fire*), shown in Ex. 6. Clapton's wah timing seems deliberately irregular, but you can perfect this difficult technique by practicing wah pulses in steady eighth notes, eighth-note triplets, and six-teenth-notes against a metronome pulse. When timed, the effect sounds like exaggerated amp tremolo. Try approximating the overstated tremolo effect from the Tommy James & The Shondells' 1960s bubblegum fave "Crimson and Clover" by wiggling the wah in regular six-teenth-notes over a I-V-IV-V progression such as *G-D-C-D*.

Ex. 6

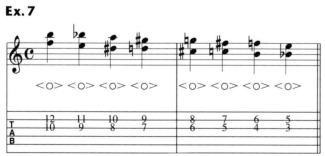

Swelling into each note is a relatively easy move that you can practice with any melody. But just for fun, try wahing into each of the descending tritones in Ex. 7, a yuk-yuk signifier common to cartoon soundtracks. Attacking a note with the wah in maximum open/treble position and then quickly "gulping" down into closed position is a bit trickier; it sounds good paired with quick descending slides like those in Ex. 8.

Actually, Ex. 8 touches on one of the most fascinating aspects of wah playing: the *relationship* between tone (as determined by the wah) and pitch. The bluesy licks in Ex. 9 develop this idea a bit more. Notes that are bent upwards are

Ex. 7

Ex. 8

paired with opening of the wah, reverse bends with closings. Psychoacoustically speaking, we seem to want to correlate brightness of tone with highness of pitch. Try experimenting with the opposite arrangement by reversing the wah moves Ex. 9. It may feel strange, but there are probably some great possibilities there.

Wah at its baddest. To see how perfectly pitch, tone, articulation, and timbre can interact, let's turn to the work of the players I consider to be wah's supreme wonder workers: not guitarists, but the horn geniuses of Duke Ellington's '20s

Ex. 9
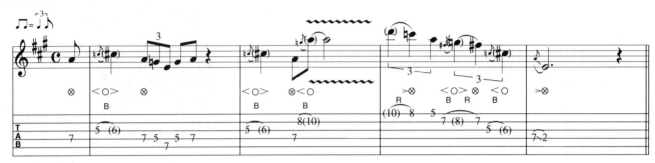

and '30s bands. Trumpeters Bubber Miley and Cootie Williams and trombonist Tricky Sam Nanton created sublime wah effects by working rubber plunger caps against the bells of their horns. Their wah inflections, lip slurs, glissandos, and "growl" effects mesh in endlessly subtle and varied ways. Ex. 10 is a very crude approximation of the sort of blues licks Miley played on Ellington's first great recording, 1926's "East St. Louis Toodle-O." (The ultracool Vocalion Records version is included on a Decca CD, *Duke Ellington and His Orchestra: The Brunswick Era Vol. 1*, alongside other unspeakably great performances.)

Note how Miley uses devices rarely attempted by guitarists, such as rapidly alternating "open" and "closed" versions of the same pitch (an effect we can heighten by playing the pitch on different strings, as in measures 1, 2, and 6). Also note the great variation in the rate of wah application — everything from instant back-and-forth to gradual swells. There's never a false move, and certainly none of the nervous fidgeting you hear from less-than-experienced wah-wrangling six-stringers. (And remember, our crude notation doesn't capture the gradations between the full-open and full-closed positions.)

Ex. 10

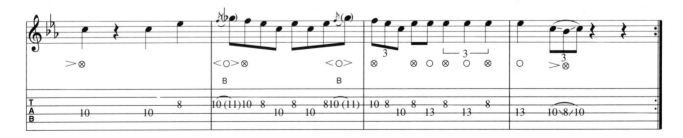

The Complete Song Transcription!
"N.S.U."
By Jack Bruce

TEXT BY JESSE GRESS

The traditional opening song during the early days of Cream, Jack Bruce's "N.S.U." soon became a vehicle for the band's legendary extended improvisations. Though less solo-laden than the shorter, more concise studio version found on "Fresh Cream," it remains to this day a textbook example of excellence in composition and performance.

Eric Clapton's simple arpeggiated figure emphasizes a C pedal tone on all off-beat eighth notes that both complements and contrasts Bruce's against-the-grain vocal melody and bass line. Five bars into each verse, E.C. backs up Bruce's Wagnerian vocal excursions with thick descending power chords voiced with the 5th in the bass. An overdubbed second guitar plays short stabs of double- and triple-stops built on the same voicings. Clapton also sings the lower vocal harmony.

E.C.'s milky 12-bar solo soars over a two-guitar backdrop in which one holds a feedback-driven 5th position *A* chord and the other pounds an identical voicing with the first and second strings added. For melodic grist, Clapton mills through the *A* pentatonic minor possibilities in the 5th, 8th, and 12th positions. Notice how his use of space is as important as the notes themselves. I've always taken particular delight in E.C.'s use of string "zips" (as in bar 58) preceding or following phrases. The licks in bars 59-62 take on an almost conversational quality that doesn't completely transfer to paper, so listen closely for those subtle, soul-searching moments.

N.S.U.

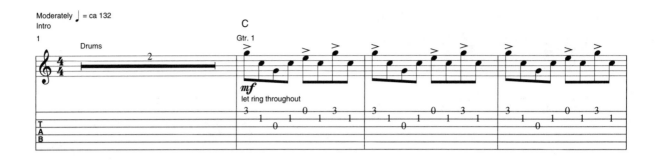

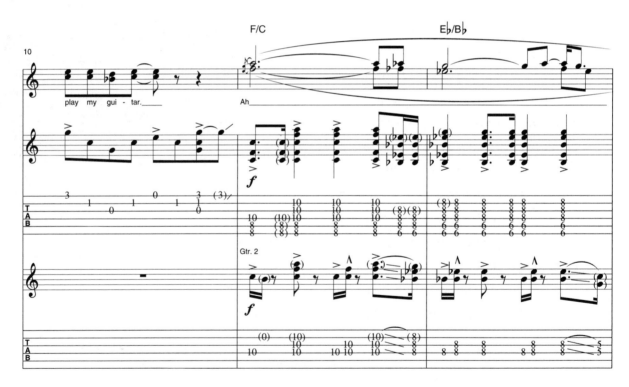

N.S.U. Words and Music by Jack Bruce, Copyright © 1968 by Dratleaf, Ltd. (PRS),
All rights administered by Chappell & Co., International Copyright Secured, All Rights Reserved

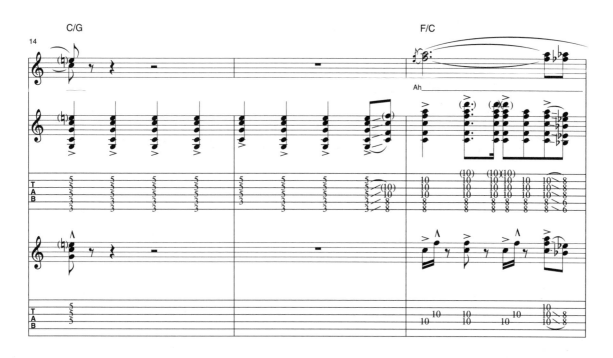

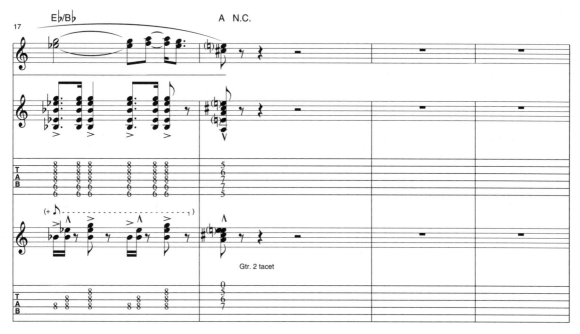

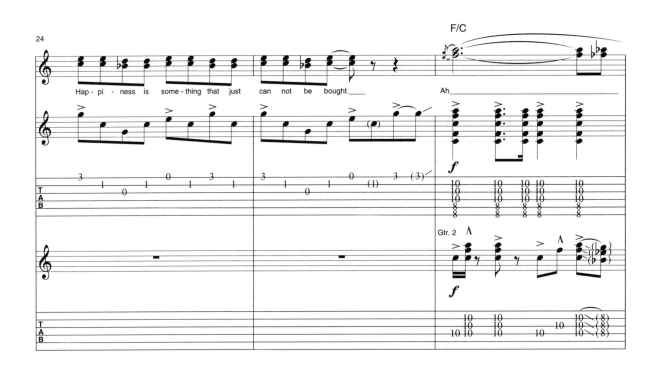

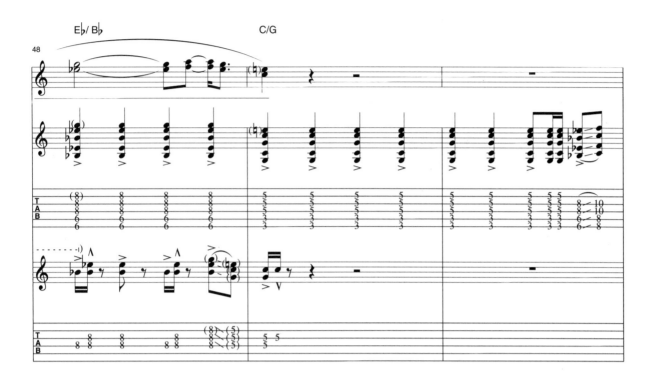

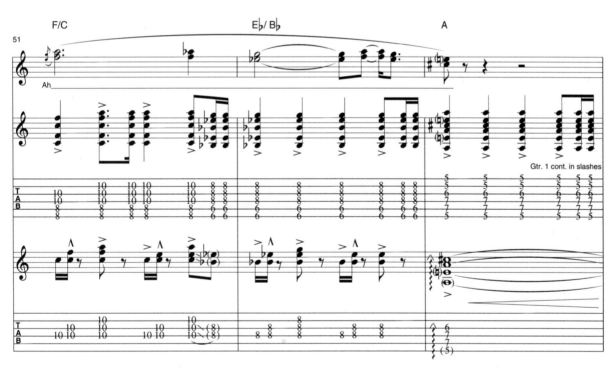

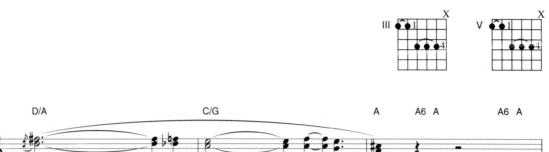

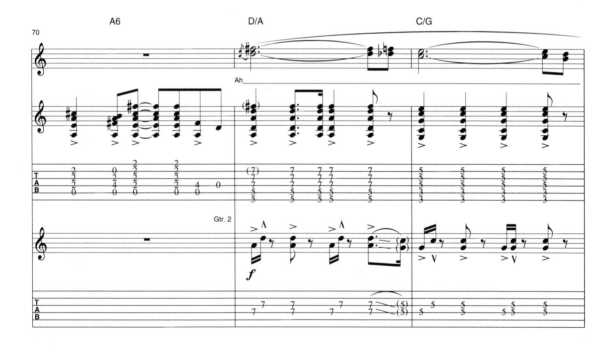

N.S.U.

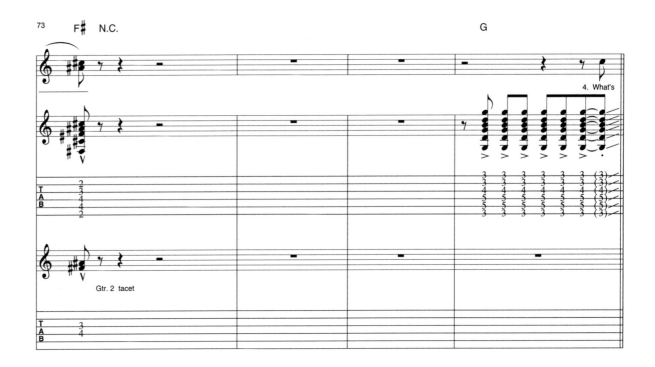

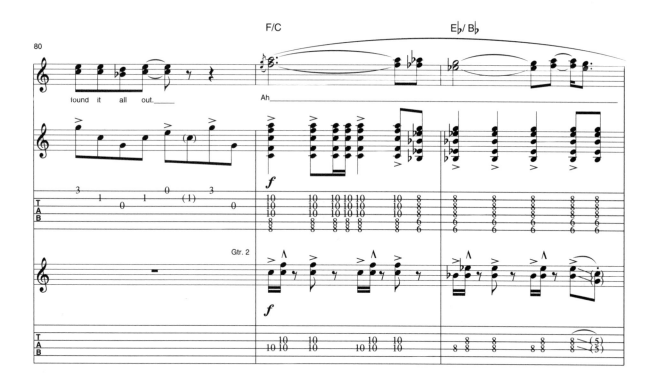

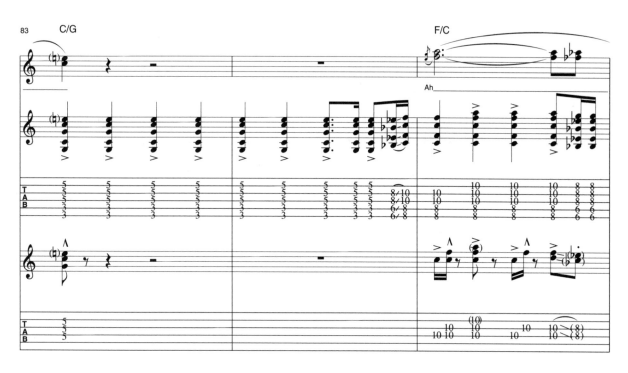

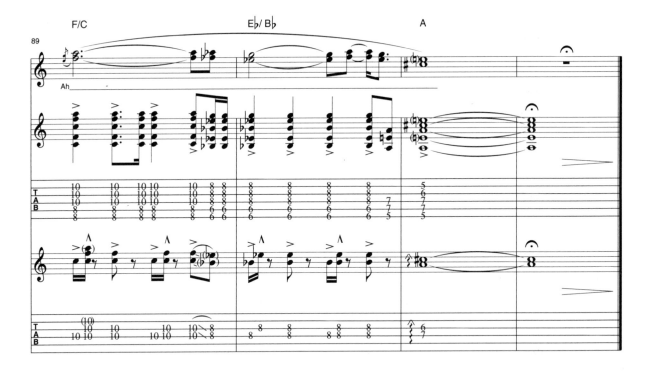

Where There's Smoke...
The Licks That Stoked Deep Purple's Fire

BY JESSE GRESS

Ritchie Blackmore may be the missing link between the great blues-based rockers of the '60s and the diatonic shredders of the '80s. The unique hybrid of blues-rock idioms and quasi-classical modal and harmonic minor sounds that he developed during his years with Deep Purple and Rainbow grew out of Hendrix, Page, and Beck while anticipating Van Halen, Malmsteen, and their countless imitators.

Influenced by Big Jim Sullivan, Scotty Moore, James Burton, Duane Eddy, and Les Paul, Blackmore started out as a session player with the Outlaws and Screaming Lord Sutch before joining the original Deep Purple lineup in 1968. The band's early-'70s incarnation may have been *the* prototype heavy metal band. Their *In Rock*, *Fireball*, *Machine Head*, and *Made In Japan* albums, all recorded between '70 and '73, remain landmarks of the genre epitomized to this day by the Blackmore power chords that open "Smoke On The Water."

Long identified as a Strat cat, Blackmore actually used a Gibson ES-335 on the first two Purple albums before making the switch midway through the third and embarking on his radical tremolo bar approach. He also switched from Vox AC30 amps to customized Marshalls that he claimed pushed 500-plus watts. (Did I mention that Ritchie likes it loud?)

Blackmore says a year of early classical training influenced his compositional sense and contributed to the extraordinary dexterity

TRACK 9

of his left-hand pinky. But structured study never diminished Blackmore's penchant for musical risk-taking. "The art of chance music is knowing what to do if you don't get what you first tried for," he told *Guitar Player* back in 1972. "That's what interests me — playing with electricity."

The following examples show some of Blackmore's favorite musical building blocks. Ex. 1a illustrates how Ritchie favors spicing up pentatonic minor runs with the #4/♭5 scale degree, often hitting the note straight on rather than bending into it. The ♮6 gives the bluesy lick in Ex. 1b a Dorian slant.

Another passing tone, the ♭7 (*A*), appears in Ex. 2, which combines all of the above elements to lead into an introductory V chord. The brief

Ex. 1a

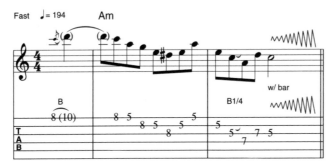

Ex. 1b

Ex. 2

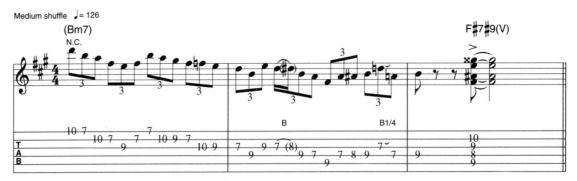

bend into the ♮3rd (D#) blurs the line between major and minor. In fact the only missing chromatic scale degrees are ♭2, ♮2, and ♭6. Ex. 3 has a definite Dorian vibe, but also emphasizes #4 (E#). And ♭2, a darker Phrygian element, appears briefly in Ex. 4.

The short *A* minor ostinatos in Examples 5a through 5c appear often in Blackmore solos. Ritchie is also fond of moving the entire patterns (especially 5c) up and down the neck in half-steps. The bluesy riff in Ex. 5d introduces a rhythmic variation, while Ex. 5e adds the Aeolian/natural minor ♭6 (*F*).

Ex. 3

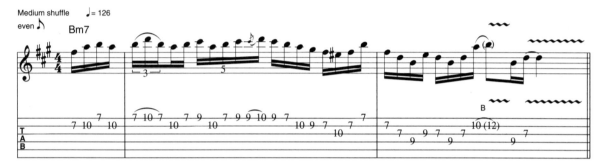

Ex. 4

Ex. 5a   Ex. 5b   Ex. 5c

Ex. 5d   Ex. 5e

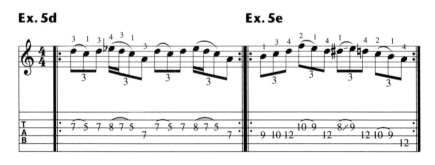

The pure *A* Phrygian run in Ex. 6 makes a great pinky-development exercise. The minor/add 9 arpeggio and ensuing bend in Ex. 7 lead to a cross-rhythm figure that momentarily implies 3/8 time. And Blackmore plays the ascending triplet arpeggios in Ex. 8 using strict alternate picking — no easy feat. Try harmonizing this line in diatonic thirds and fifths.

Ex. 6

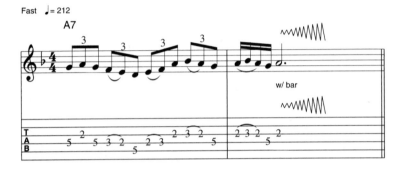

Ex. 7

Ex. 8

The descending arpeggios in Ex. 9 incorporate bends into a Bach-influenced progression. Ex. 10 treats the same progression with a speedy, ascending motif that works its way up the E string diatonically, then descends via chromatic pull-offs over an open-E pedal. Again, Blackmore's alternate picking approaches the superhuman.

Ex. 9

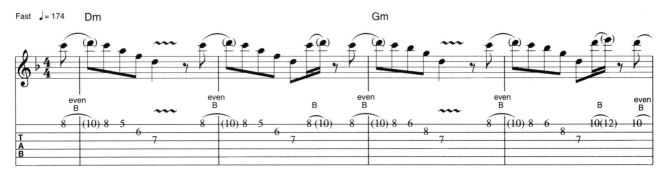

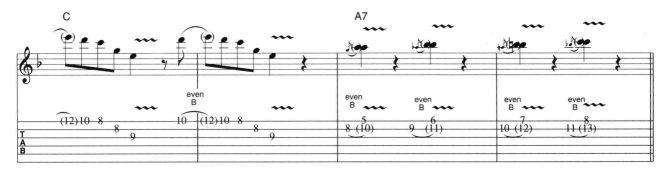

Ex. 10

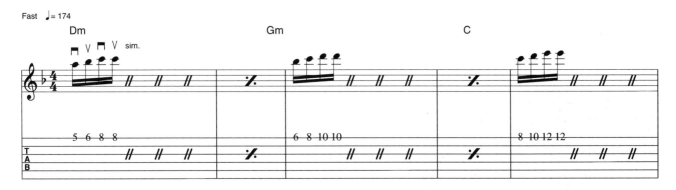

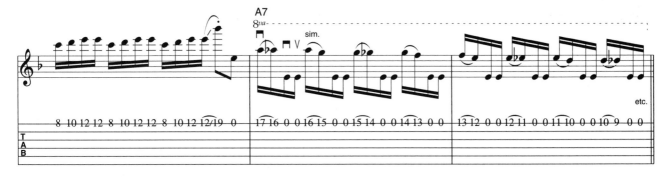

A Gypsy-flavored ensemble line from the Rainbow era, Ex. 11 relies entirely on the *E* harmonic minor scale to play through the V-i progression. (The Phrygian dominant mode, beloved by '80s neo-classical rockers, is built from the 5th scale degree of the harmonic minor scale.) The first two bars of Ex. 12 outline i and iv of *G* minor, blending *G* Aeolian and blues lines before shifting to *C* Aeolian and harmonic minor ideas. Ritchie treats each chord separately; *C* minor becomes a temporary tonal center, not just the subdominant of *G* minor. The cool *D7* arpeggiations in bar 3 come from the *G* harmonic minor scale. The ♭2nd/♭9th degree (*E♭*) adds extra tension, and the concluding phrase is pure Bach 'n' roll.

Ex. 11

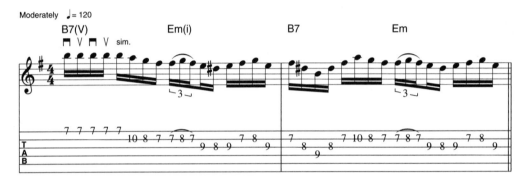

Ex. 12

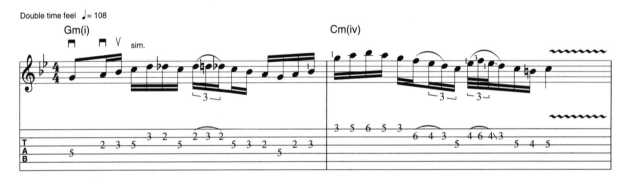

Ex. 13

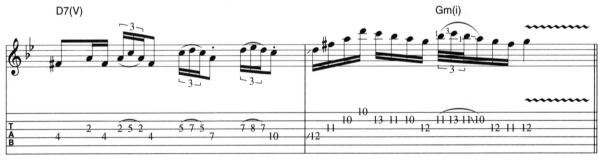

Texas Chainsaw Lead Guitar

A Lesson with Eric Johnson

BY JIM FERGUSON

With influences ranging from Jimi Hendrix and Jeff Beck to Jerry Reed and Chet Atkins to Wes Montgomery and Lenny Breau, Eric Johnson takes a progressive approach to nearly everything he plays. When it comes to bluesy rock, he can tear into a chord pattern with aggressive single-note lines like a chainsaw chewing through balsa wood. We asked Eric to detail his playing, and his responses will help you master blues-rock without massacring it.

Great players can smoothly integrate chords and single notes, putting more adjectives in their playing and coloring it up more. Wes Montgomery and Jimi Hendrix were especially good at this, but pedal steel and country guitarists also do it well, approaching a tune from several angles at once. Combining chords and single notes adds a lot of feeling to whatever you play because it creates a potent yin-yang tension.

Of course you don't always have to mix chords and leads; how much you do it depends on the music. But being very familiar with a progression helps you select single notes with a lot more purpose, making you a much more effective, well-rounded player.

This lesson is based on a common *E-A* pattern that I play with pick-and-fingers technique. The feel is similar in concept to "Steve's Boogie" [from *Tones,* Reprise]. First let's look at a few variations on the chords, and then talk about a variety of ways I'd approach it from a single-note standpoint. Throughout, remember that the material is

TRACK 10

interchangeable, and parts of the chordal examples and single-note licks can be freely mixed together.

Chords In The Pocket. The basic chords (Ex. 1) should be played at about 112 bpm. The last beat of measure 2 suggests *D*, a common extension of the pattern. Notice that the 3rd is left out of each chord, producing a characteristic rock sound.

I use pick-and-fingers technique for the chords, but you can also play them fingerstyle, palming the pick. Regardless of the approach, the chords are spread across the six strings, so give your right hand some time to feel comfortable with skipping strings.

Ex. 2 elaborates on Ex. 1 with single notes from the *E* minor pentatonic scale, and has another way of suggesting the *D* chord in measure 2. Play Ex. 2 with a driving feel. Also try it with Ex. 1's *D* lick plugged into measure 2.

Fingerpicking plays more of a role in Ex. 3, where your right hand should kind of rock back and forth between the sixth, fourth, and first strings. When you get this under your fingers, work on spontaneously mixing up the notes and even applying some Travis picking patterns.

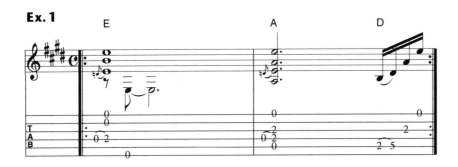

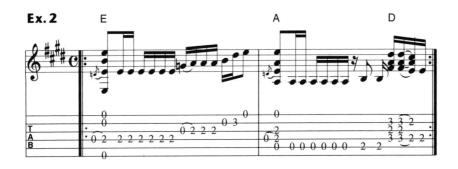

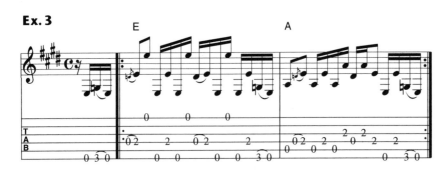

The bass line in the first measure of Ex. 4 adds variety by breaking things up; with the exception of the low *G#*, every note is from the *E* minor pentatonic scale. Measure 2 features a country blues-type lick based on *A7* that makes a nice change of pace from the *A* chord treatment in the previous examples.

Scales, Licks, & Bends. Scalewise, I'd approach this *E-A* pattern like the first part of "Cliffs Of Dover" [from *Tones*] — with the *E* minor pentatonic scale. Ex. 5 shows a common pattern I use for breaking up pentatonics. Notice that I start in the 12th position and move down to the seventh, where you can end with either the low or fifth string *E*. Ex. 6 reverses the pattern and goes from the 7th fret area up to the 12th. These fingerings work well for long single-note ideas. So you can better hear how the scale works over the progression, Ex. 7 puts the pattern in the form of a lick and ends with the *A* chord.

Ex. 4

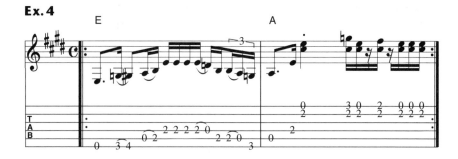

Ex. 5

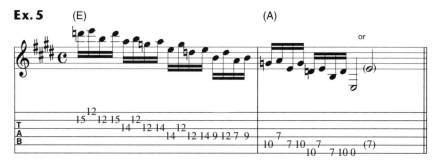

Ex. 6

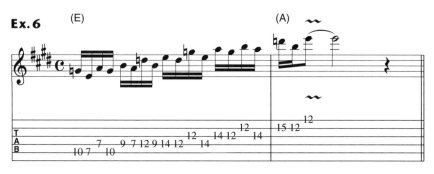

Ex. 7

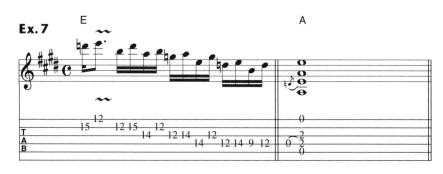

Any pentatonic scale can produce limitless phrases. In Ex. 8, I use a short riff to tie the E and A chords together. Notice how the quick hammers and pulls add expression and that the notes fit each chord, even though they're all from the E minor pentatonic.

A number of notes can be used to color a pentatonic scale. One of my favorites is the ♭5, or B♭

for E minor pentatonic. Ex. 9 shows a quick B♭ pull-off and moves from the 5th fret down to the 2nd, while Ex. 10 uses a hammer/pull combination and a rhythm with eighth- and sixteenth-notes.

Depending on the situation, you can put an adjective in your blues or rock playing by bending almost any pentatonic note. The lowered 7th is stretched up to the root in Ex. 11, resulting in a

Ex. 8

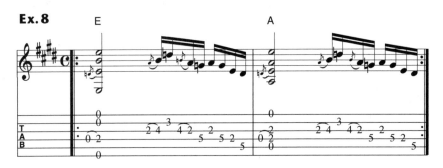

Ex. 9

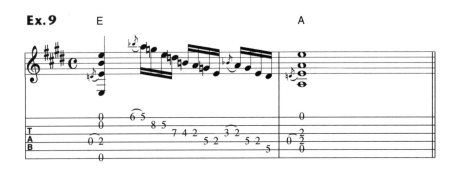

Ex. 10

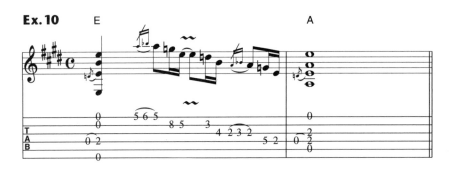

Ex. 11

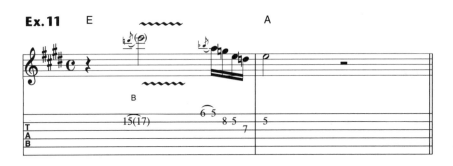

classic rock sound. (I follow this with Ex. 9's *B♭* pull-off.) While Ex. 11's bend happens on the second beat of the measure, Ex. 12's is on the first beat.

Another common bend goes from the pentatonic's lowered 3rd up to the 4th. Ex. 13 and Ex. 14 show the *G♮* pushed to *A.* In each case the bend is in the same part of the measure but is followed with a different pentatonic idea.

Always beginning a melodic idea on the same beat can result in predictable playing. Ex. 15 shows a phrase that acts as a pickup, leading to the *E* chord. Also notice that the bend goes from *F♯* to *G* — the 2nd (or 9th) up to the lowered 3rd.

Ex. 16 and Ex. 17 show another classic rock bend, stretching the 4th up a whole tone — *A* up to *B,* in *E* pentatonic. In Ex. 16 the bend happens on the first beat, while in Ex. 17 it's on the second.

Ex. 12

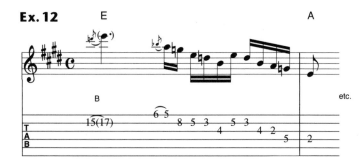

Ex. 13   **Ex. 14**

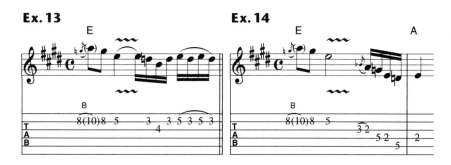

Ex. 15   **Ex. 16**

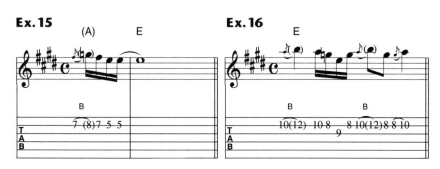

Ex. 17

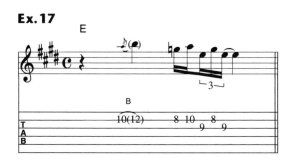

Sometimes I like to bend the ♭3 up to ♮3, as in Ex. 18. In this case, go up just shy of the *G#,* a quality I especially like. Here I've also added another note — the 6th, or *C#.* I wouldn't necessarily use this phrase in a rock tune, but it's very effective for country or blues.

For single-note work I use alternate up/down strokes for the most part, but don't let that discourage you from working on these single-note ideas with sweep technique. Also experiment with adding hammer-ons and pull-offs to scales, which can add a flowing quality to your leads.

Two-Note Ideas. This article mainly concentrates on chordal and single-note playing, but there are a lot of other possibilities, including two-note lines. While Ex. 19 reminds me of something Jerry Reed might do, it can still be combined with our first four examples.

In general, I like to keep pairs of notes moving along fairly quickly; if they remain stationary for too long they can start to suggest chords you don't intend. For example, notice how the second part of Ex. 19's second beat implies the *D* chord, while the first part of the third beat is similar to the *A* chord.

Getting it Together. Once you've learned each example, work on interchanging them while maintaining the feel of the two-measure *E-A* pattern. Then vary the ideas and begin to add new ones, making the material your own. Finally, learn all scales, chords, and licks in as many fretboard locations as possible and absorb all the theory you can — it'll help you label ideas, see how they work, and prevent you from becoming a Festus of the guitar!

Ex. 18

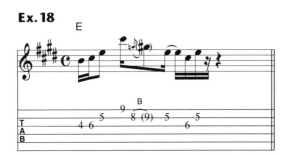

Ex. 19

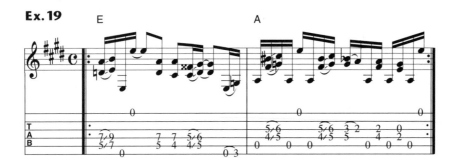

Soaring with Skydog
Duane Allman

BY JESSE GRESS

 quarter century after his passing, Duane Allman remains the unsurpassed king of rock slide guitar. Already steeped in the blues of Muddy Waters, Howlin' Wolf, Willie Dixon, B.B. King, Eric Clapton, and Jeff Beck, Duane became enamored with slide after hearing the late Jesse Ed Davis perform Blind Willie McTell's "Statesboro Blues" with Taj Mahal at an L.A. club. Using a glass bottle for a slide, Duane also began emulating Little Walter, Sonny Boy Williamson, and other blues harmonica players. In time, even his non-slide playing took on characteristics of his bottleneck style, as if both were becoming melded into one voice.

Duane was obviously a fast learner with an uncanny grasp of open-*E* tuning, as heard on his records with the Allman Brothers Band and his soulful backing of Wilson Pickett, Aretha Franklin, King Curtis, John Hammond, Boz Scaggs, Clarence Carter, and others. Though he began playing bottleneck in standard tuning, Allman preferred open *E*, and he eventually limited his standard-tuned slide excursions to songs like "Dreams" and "Mountain Jam."

Early in 1970 the Brothers cut a studio version of "Statesboro Blues" in the key of *C*, while the later live *At The Fillmore* version was in *D*. A few months later, during the recording of *Idlewild South*, Allman tracked more cutting-edge, open-*E*-tuned electric slide on "Don't Keep Me Wonderin'" and "One More Ride." Continuing his session work, he began to hit his stride later that year during Eric Clapton's *Layla* sessions. His bottleneck ranged from subdued to incendiary on eight of these tracks, almost all of which are in open *E* ("Layla" and "I Am Yours" are the exceptions). The *Layla* outtake "Mean Old World," a dobro duet with E.C., is perhaps Duane's only recording in the more rural open-*G* tuning. Duane's next big project, the Brothers' *At Fillmore East*, represents the pinnacle of bottleneck performance, *the* book of electric slide.

Gear-wise, Duane favored Les Pauls, 50-watt Marshalls, and a glass Coricidin bottle worn over his ring finger. While sliding, he used his right-hand

TRACK 11

thumb, index, and middle fingers, which served double duty damping unwanted strings. Duane also used his left-hand middle and index fingers to damp behind the bottle. Low frets and medium-high action were also helpful. For accuracy like Duane's, align the tip of your ring finger directly over the fret.

Guitarists commonly use bends, hammer-ons, pull-offs, and finger slides to get from one note to the next. The slide imposes limitations on these techniques but offers several alternatives. In Ex. 1a both notes are fretted with the slide with no audible glissando in between. Ex. 1b features a picked grace-note slide into the second note, a motion performed with a single pick attack in Ex. 1c. Think blues harp for the even gliss in Ex. 1d. The grace-note slide preceding the first note of each previous example adds even more smoky harmonica flavor.

The advantages of open-*E* tuning are increased string tension (for more sustain) and economy of

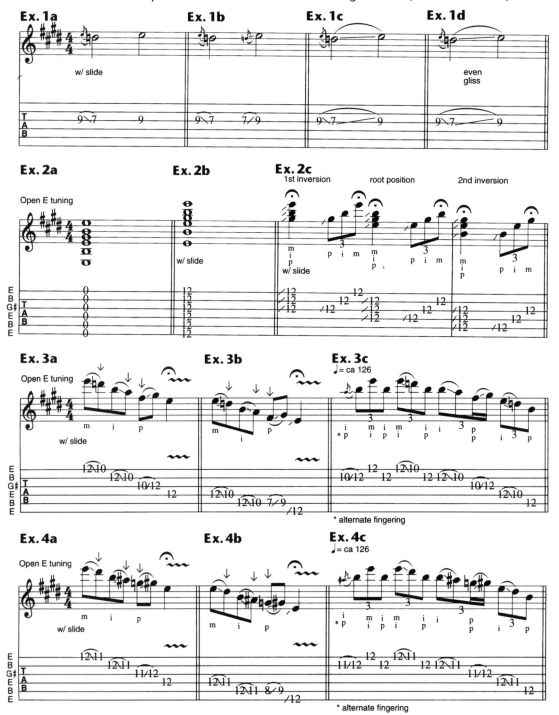

motion. Raising the open fifth and fourth strings a whole-step and the third string a half-step produces an open E chord (Ex. 2a), giving you, from low to high, the root, 5, root, 3, 5, and root. Since the root positions on the sixth and first strings remain unaffected, it's not necessary to relearn notes when moving the chord shape around the fingerboard. Using the slide to barre all six strings, this chord voicing may be transposed to 11 other fret positions to accommodate chord changes or playing in different keys before recycling an octave higher (Ex. 2b). Open-E tuning also offers easy access to all three triad inversions, playable as chords or arpeggios. Ex. 2c demonstrates this while summarizing Duane's right-hand technique. For arpeggios, begin with the fingers resting on the strings as if you were about to play the entire chord, and then pluck each note individually.

When it came to spinning single-note lines (which made up 99 percent of his slide work), Duane preferred the urban "box" approach over more traditional open-string stylings. The box shape is formed by the addition of neighbor tones below the tonic chord position. Ex. 3a and Ex. 3b illustrate the lower neighbors (notated below the downward arrow) a whole-step below each chord tone. These lower neighbors (the lowered 7, 4, and 2/9) are incorporated in a typical Duane-style lick in Ex. 3c. Ex. 4a and Ex. 4b show the chromatic half-step neighbors (the natural 7, raised 4/lowered 5, and lowered 3), while Ex. 4c adapts them to the previous lick. In Ex. 5 the same lick is treated to a combination of whole-step and chromatic lower neighbors.

Be sure to explore another important element of Duane's sound, the world of sweet'n'sour microtones present between neighbor tones. Transpose these ideas over the entire fingerboard. Remember, Duane played fluently in any key.

The next examples cover some of the building blocks of Duane's style. Each motif stands on its own and may be developed in many ways, including repetition, rhythmic displacement, elongation, and retrograde (reversing the order of the notes). Ex. 6a features a four-note motif moving across adjacent string groups with whole-step lower neighbors. Ex. 6b shows what a difference a subtle change in phrasing can make. Examples 7a through

Ex. 5

Ex. 6a

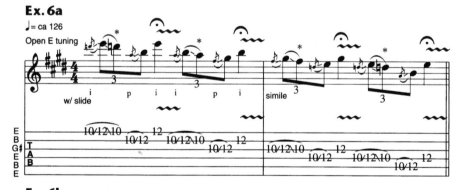

Ex. 6b

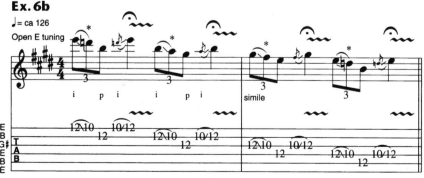

7d follow the same logic using a five-note motif. For some astonishing variations, replace the whole-step lower neighbors marked by asterisks with chromatic neighbors or in-between microtones.

Neighbors *above* the tonic chord include the 2nd/9th, 6th, and 4th scale degrees. Duane used these sparingly, mostly as grace-note slides or for an occasional splash of pentatonic-major color.

Instead, he'd extend the box by momentarily zipping up a major 3rd on the first or fourth strings, or by using the important minor-third spacing (only found between the second or third strings) to create a dominant 7th chord fragment three frets above the tonic. In the key of *E*, sliding up three frets from the tonic's *G* and *B* yields *B* and *D♯*, part of the E7 chord (Ex. 8a). Ex. 8b shows the

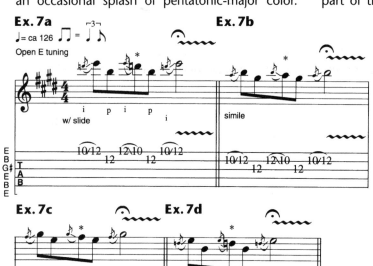

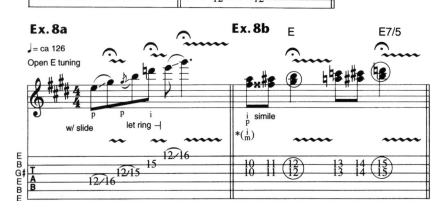

* alternate fingering

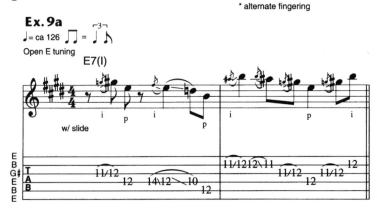

whole-step and chromatic neighbor possibilities for both two-note structures.

Culled from medium-tempo shuffles, Examples 9a through 10b capture some of Duane's signature phrases. All have been transposed to *E* for mixin' and matchin'. Ex. 9a is very harmonica-like. Add even more sass by exploiting those microtones. Ex. 9b uses the implied 7th chord described above, and then outlines a descending box combining whole- and half-step lower neighbors. Ex. 9c's chromatically ascending minor thirds lead up to a signature major third jump up the first string before the descending box/octave-leap conclusion. A similar move in Ex. 10 navigates the IV-1 change, as does Ex. 10b, a funky mid-register harp lick.

Transposed to the key of *D*, the blues harp outing in Ex. II covers the last four measures of a 12-bar blues. Duane's flawless intonation is evident as he zips off the fingerboard to the hypothetical 26th fret. Move it up a whole step (to *E*) for a real trip into the stratosphere.

When bottlenecking in standard tuning, Duane often wove adventurous linear excursions up and down the string in place of the blues-box approach, perhaps partially influenced by his interest in jazz greats Miles Davis and John Coltrane. Duane's melodic development is masterful in Ex. 12, inspired by a videotaped performance of "Dreams." His two-bar call-and-response lines emphasize a 3/4 pulse, while the rhythm section lays down a 6/8 jazz waltz.

Ex. 9b

Ex. 9c

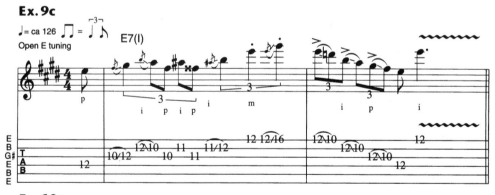

Ex. 10a

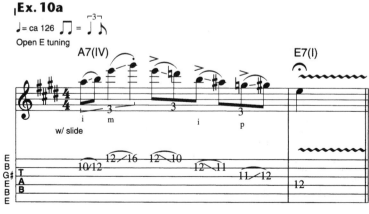

Ex. 10b

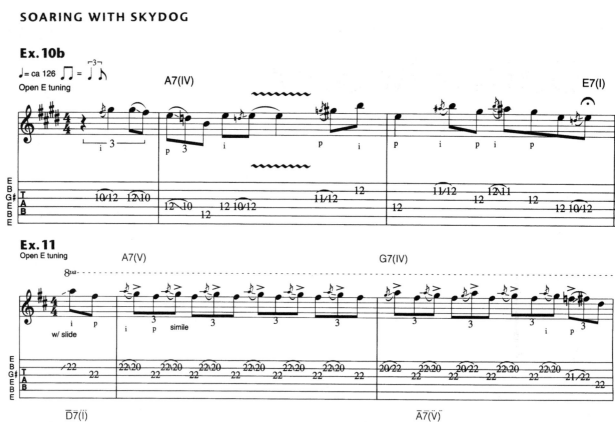

Ex. 11

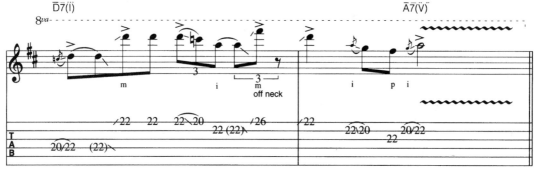

Ex. 12

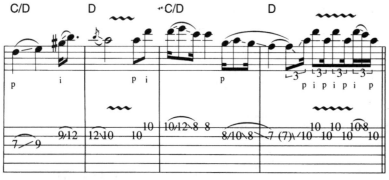

Guitar Repair
Do It Yourself?!

BY DAN ERLEWINE

uitarists tend to regard an instrument as something sacred. You've spent a lot of money for it, and it does seem sort of complicated if you don't know much about it. While repairmen are always happy to get your business, there are plenty of little "repairs," maintenance tasks actually, that you can do yourself—you shouldn't be afraid of your instrument. Serious players typically spend hours tweaking the action on their guitars.

One of the best ways to avoid repair bills is to spend more time buying the guitar in the first place. Instead of spending $2,500 for six different guitars before you finally get your first good one, learn more about it and buy the best guitar you can afford to start with.

When you go to buy an acoustic guitar, for example, take along a mirror so you can look inside and see how well the guitar is built. If you are dealing with a quality instrument, you can expect to find good workmanship, but people who buy cheaper guitars (usually imports) sometimes have problems with them because they didn't check out what they were buying.

You're pretty safe with a brand-name guitar, but you should read every article you can get your hands on. It would be smart to buy a guitar repair book before you go shopping. I'm thinking in particular of both volumes of Don Teeter's *The Acoustic Guitar* (University of Oklahoma Press) and Hideo Kamimoto's *Guitar Repair* (Oak Publications), and of course my own *Guitar Player Repair Guide* (Miller Freeman).

Learn how guitars are built so you'll recognize such things as warped necks, loose frets, and loose braces. How many people do you know who bought a guitar and afterward wish they hadn't? Even some brand-name guitars are made with unseasoned wood and develop problems which cause them to play poorly, so buyer beware!

Adjusting a truss rod. Anyone who can operate a microwave or a CD player should be able to adjust a neck rod by using a little common sense and reading up on the task at hand. Simple tools like Allen wrenches, nut drivers, and screwdrivers are all that's needed, but study the books to find out what sizes and to learn which way to turn the adjusting nut! As a rule, if you tighten the nut, the neck will straighten out. If you go the other way, it will loosen up and go with the pull of the strings (introducing "relief" into the fretboard). You shouldn't be afraid to do this.

Some necks play their best when adjusted perfectly straight; others need a small amount of "relief" to give the string extra clearance over the fret tops—especially toward the center of the string's vibration arc-to keep from buzzing. So if you sight down the neck from the nut towards the body and see a little dip in there around the 9th or 10th fret, it's probably relief. My personal choice is a rather straight neck on any guitar unless there are buzzes that I can't play around or remove by fret leveling. When all else fails, I'll adjust a little relief into the neck as a last resort—again, this is a personal choice.

Replacing tuners. This falls under the category of something you shouldn't do yourself, unless you're installing exact retro-fit tuners. In the shop we see too many cracked pegheads where people have tried to drill out the hole with a hand drill. The best way to do it is to use a clamp and drill press or a hand reamer and round file.

Don't oil your tuning pegs. Oil seeps through the screw holes that hold the tuner and into the back of the peghead, causing swelling of the wood and even splits or cracks. Most modern tuners are permanently lubricated, sealed, and shouldn't be oiled anyway. If you have open-gear tuners that are stiff, smear a tiny bit of petroleum jelly onto the gears.

Cleaning the fretboard. I don't use any spray or stick lubricants on the fretboard, and never have—I find them much too slippery. I prefer simply to keep the fretboard and strings clean. Clean the fretboard periodically with a dry rag. If the frets are well seated, there's no reason you can't use a

damp (not wet!) rag and soap to loosen grime—soap and water can clean anything on a guitar if you're careful, especially on an electric. If there's too much built-up dirt, use some extra fine (0000) steel wool pressed into the edge of the fret with your thumbnail. Occasionally, perhaps once or twice a year, work a small amount of lemon oil into the fretboard. Don't put anything on maple fretboards, because they're lacquered. Use only cloth to clean them—steel wool will scratch.

As for removing all the strings to clean the fretboard, it does upset the tension balance on an acoustic guitar, but it's not a big deal with electric guitars. When I'm removing strings on a delicate vintage acoustic guitar, I prefer to introduce the loss of tension gradually by detuning slowly. I tune down to *D* and play it for a while, and then tune down to *C* and play it, and finally remove the strings.

When you change strings, adjust a truss rod, or do anything to a good-playing guitar (especially acoustics), expect to wait a few days for the instrument to settle back into peak playing form. A smart repairman gets a guitar done days before the customer comes to pick it up, so it will sound at least as good as it did when they brought it in, hopefully better.

Nuts. The setup of the nut and bridge have a great effect on your guitar's sound and playability. It's hard to make a good nut, and it takes some time, so don't expect your repair shop to just pull one out of a drawer and send you off down the street.

Each string should come up gradually over the nut and have its contact point right at the front of the nut. With most factory nuts and nuts from a drawer at a music store, you can't even tell where the string is contacting because it's down too deep in the groove.

You want the string slots to angle slightly towards the pegs, so that the string will go where it naturally wants to lie. I like to relieve the sides of my nut grooves away from the string, so they are not pinching and muting it. You need a lot of different size files to make nuts (Stewart-MacDonald has a good starter set).

A really nice nut won't last forever. If you hone it down carefully, so it's comfortable to play in the first position but doesn't buzz, it will wear out in time, regardless of the material it's made of. You'll have to shim it up or have another nut made. If your nut makes a "chinking" sound when you tune, and you're unable to smooth and shape a slot that's pinching a string, lubricate it with a little petroleum jelly or Teflon-lube.

Bridge setup. You'll be happiest if you learn to adjust your own intonation, because it's not something you do only once in a lifetime (each change in string gauge usually requires a readjustment of the bridge saddles). After all, it's your own ear you're tuning to, right? My ear is different from yours. I can make a guitar play really in tune, and when I go out and play a job, it sounds great to me. But that doesn't mean that you'd like it.

Make this adjustment on each string: If the string notes sharp when you compare the fretted note at the 12th fret with the open harmonic at the 12th fret, move the individual saddle back, away from the neck; if the string notes flat, adjust the saddle forward.

It's easy to clean the bridge parts on most electric guitars. Take the bridge apart and clean the pieces with naphtha or lighter fluid. Get all the grease off the parts, put them back together, then lightly lubricate any working surfaces with thin oil (sewing machine oil is nice), and your bridge will work well again.

As for substituting one type of bridge for another, you should avoid pulling bridge studs and moving bridge parts around, like trying to put a tune-o-matic on a guitar that doesn't have one. And be very careful when putting a stop tailpiece on an ES-335 that has a trapeze on it—you might install it crooked. Take that job to a pro.

Most bridge inserts, or "saddles," have pretty rough castings—they're not machined perfectly, and the string slots are filed quickly at the factory. Many people have to replace the bridge pieces on their brand new guitars because the string spacings aren't right, or the strings are too close to the edge of the fretboard, or they don't go over the polepieces properly, or they break easily. Most Fender-style bridge saddles don't require string slots because they're cast into the saddle. Gibson Tune-O-Matic-style bridges usually require a slot to be cut into the insert.

Simply changing bridge saddles isn't very hard. Buy a new set of saddles, take your bridge apart, put the pieces on, and reset the intonation. If your guitar plays in good tune before you remove the saddles, make a note of each saddle location so you can return to it with the new saddles. If you're replacing the Gibson style saddles, which need slots cut, buy a little set of needle files to cut the slots, and some 400- or 600-grade sandpaper to smooth the slots when you're done filing.

Although most tremolo adjustments are fairly easy, they're beyond the scope of this article. In brief, keep any friction points clean and lubricated with a light grease. To keep a tremolo guitar with a traditional (non-locking) nut in tune, you must have a properly made nut that doesn't pinch the strings.

There's not much I can say about acoustic bridges here—the subject is too deep, so read some books! I don't recommend do-it-yourselfers attempt bridge repairs on a flat-top guitar. If you can remove the saddle and would like to reshape it, that's fine (it's sort of like slotting your own electric bridge saddles), but don't attempt to remove or reglue a bridge—take that to a pro.

Keep an eye on the back edge of an acoustic bridge; if it's coming loose, you'll see the gap between the bridge and the top. Take a string envelope and try to slide the flap under any part of the bridge. If you can slip it under there, you better get it checked out. We see lots of bridges that could have been fixed more easily (sometimes better) when they first started coming loose.

Don't fret. Refretting and dressing frets is the most important job a repairman can do. Like bridge regluing, this is something you shouldn't try yourself. And before you have your frets dressed or redone, spend some time trying different string gauges to find out what you really like. Then be sure the repairman knows what brand of strings you use—that's critical. If you get a refret and setup, and then drastically change string gauges, it's not going to play the same without a fresh setup.

I fret guitars using a jig that puts tension on the neck and holds it at concert pitch when the strings are removed. The body is also held, so there is no spring-back. When I take strings off a Les Paul, for example, the neck will bow up a little bit because of the truss rod tension. When I loosen the rod, it sets right back down on the tension jig's neck supports. That is right about where the neck will be when you play it. Then I take the frets out and get rid of any humps or bumps by judiciously leveling the fretboard.

When compared to a straightedge, the upper register of the fretboard (from the 10th to the last fret) should be flat, or even fall slightly away from the straightedge. Many guitars "hump" a bit in that area, which causes string buzz. So there's more to a refret job than just pulling out the frets and hammering-in new ones. Put your money on a good fret job and you'll never be sorry.

Pickup adjustment. Adjusting the pickup height is definitely a job you can and should do (you've got to please yourself). Raise and lower the pickup height until you like what you hear. If you get the pickups too high you'll know it because the strings will hit them. Fender-style pickups generally have pickups without individually adjustable polepieces; Gibson-style humbuckers and "P-90"-types have polepieces which can be raised or lowered individually to accommodate different gauges and wound or unwound strings. If you have a vintage guitar with adjustable polepieces that are rusted, don't try to turn them—take it to the shop.

Adjust the height of Gibson-style pickups with both volumes wide open. Switch back and forth between pickups while adjusting the height, until the volume of both is equal. Then *back off* the neck pickup a little bit—being at the end of the string, the bridge pickup tends to be a little weaker than the neck pickup. The Gibson factory usually sets the pickups with a clearance of 3/32" on the neck pickup and 1 /16" on the bridge pickup (clearance is measured between the string, fretted at the last fret, and the top of the polepiece).

With Stratocasters, if you're willing to lower the pickups as far away from the strings as possible, they'll sound their best and you'll get more accurate noting. The magnets are so powerful that when you fret in the upper areas (especially on the

low *E* and *A* strings), the magnets pull the strings out of tune.

Acoustic guitars are more popular than ever, and there are a great number of different style pickups to amplify them. Other than certain clip-on and "soundhole" pickups, most of the better acoustic pickups (the majority are piezo-electric transducers) are mounted inside the guitar or under the bridge saddle. Acoustic guitar amplification generally requires that some sort of input jack be mounted in place of the strap button at the butt end of the guitar body Leave the saddle slot-routing, end-pin-jack-drilling, et cetera to the pros—it's too easy to ruin your guitar.

Major repairs. If you're looking at a serious repair job, get two or three estimates. See if a prospective repair shop has samples of its work around—it's often surprising what you'll find (both good and bad). People have different ways of fixing things, and I sure wouldn't send a guitar in to be repaired without knowing what the repair shop staff was planning to do. A repairman shouldn't be insulted if you get other estimates.

If you're going to have your guitar set up for you, be sure to show the repairman how you play—too often, repairmen will try to talk you into liking what *they* like. You can't just take your guitar into a shop and say "do whatever you like." To prevent those situations where the customer comes back and says, "This buzzes," and I say, "Well, look how heavy you're playing," I like to talk about it beforehand. That's something I've learned from experience.

Finally, keep a maintenance log. Write down who fixed the guitar, the date, and what was done. Ask the repairman to list any materials—especially glues or finishes—that were used; such information can be invaluable to the repair beings of the future.

By the way: You can't have the lowest action in the world, light strings, and no buzz. Good luck!

NOTES ON CALL
Learning at the Speed of Sound™

The CD accompanying this book is produced by NOTES ON CALL, specialists in producing audio versions of lessons from *Guitar Player* and other magazines. Here are just two of the many valuable instructional products available from Notes on Call:

Sound Check #2

Check out 11 of the most popular *Guitar Player* lessons on your choice of CD or cassette for just $5, including shipping and handling. Features 11 killer lessons:

1) Studio Rhythm Secrets
2) Slowhand's Blues: Eric Clapton
3) Linear vs. Crosspicked Melodies
4) The ABCs of Funk Guitar
5) Hard drivin' Double-Stops
6) Mind-Boggling Mason
7) Duke Robillard's Swinging Double-Stops
8) The Art of Linking
9) Jazz Up Your Rock Licks
10) Stratospheric Eric Johnson
11) Open Wide

Rock Solid

This great new four-part NOTES ON CALL study program (audio versions of lessons from *Guitar Player* and other magazines) features 57 lessons covering a comprehensive range of rock guitar techniques. Available on CDs and cassettes.

16 Rock Solid Instructors: Andy Aledort, Chris Amelar, Roy Ashen, Nick Bowcott, Jimmy Brown, Askold Buk, Brad Carlton, Andy Ellis, Rik Emmett, Frank Gambale, Jesse Gress, Joe Gore, Iwo Iwaszkiewicz, Patrick Mabry, James Rotundi, and Alex Skolnick.

Featuring Signature Styles of: Ritchie Blackmore, Buckethead, Carl Culpepper, Diamond Darrell, Extreme, Marty Friedman, Eric Gales, Paul Gilbert, David Grissom, Kirk Hammett, Jimi Hendrix, Eric Johnson, Mark Knopfler, Led Zeppelin, George Lynch, Megadeth, Metallica, Jimmy Page, John Petrucci, Vernon Reid, Brian Setzer, Alex Skolnick, Steve Vai, Angus Young, and more.

You'll learn techniques that employ: chordal arpeggios, string skipping, chord melody, intervallic slides, vibrato, open string licks, pull-offs, hammer-ons, bends, chromatic runs, pedal note sweep arpeggios, hybrid picking, tricky time signatures, tapping, warm-ups, stretches, slide, legato, staccato, wah-wah, double stops, triple-stops, hexatonics, position leaps, pinched harmonics whammy bar, and more.

Rock Solid: 57 lessons by 16 instructors. A Four-Part Study Program available on CDs and cassettes: each part is $14.95 on cassette or $17.95 on CD. Get all four Rock Solid collections, all tablature, all index pages, two free bonus cassettes and a binder for $59.90 on cassette or $69.90 on CD.

To order or for more information, please contact:

NOTES ON CALL

146 Second Street North, Suite 201
St. Petersburg, FL 33701
Phone (800) 222-5544
Fax (813) 823-6523

ABOUT THE AUTHORS

Ernie Rideout is the assistant editor of *Keyboard*, a world music scholar, and an active musician in the San Francisco Bay area.

Jim Ferguson has served as associate editor of *Guitar Player*, and he is also an accomplished jazz and classical guitarist

Rik Emmett, formerly the front man of the rock trio Triumph, has produced three solo albums and is currently working on a fourth, his first all-guitar instrumental recording.

Dave Rubin has performed with Chuck Berry, Screamin' Jay Hawkins, and members of James Brown's JBs. He contributes to *Guitar Player's* "Sessions" section as well as teaching guitar in New York City. His new book is *Inside the Blues: 1942-1982* (Hal Leonard).

Jesse Gress is the music editor for *Guitar Player* and recently toured with Todd Rundgren.

Joe Gore, the Senior Editor of *Guitar Player*, has toured with Tom Waits, and also backed PJ Harvey on her 1995 tour.

Dan Erlewine has written the "Repairs and Modifications" column for *Guitar Player* since 1985. At Stewart-MacDonald's Guitar Shop Supply Company in Athens, Ohio, Erlewine has headed the Guitar Repair Research and Development Team since 1986. Much of the information here was abridged from his book, *Guitar Player Repair Guide* (Miller Freeman), now in its second edition.

The CD that accompanies this book was produced by **Notes on Call** (see box at left).

Lesson tracks on the CD are performed by **Brad Carlton**, who is living proof that monster players don't all live in the big music meccas. Based in St. Petersburg, Florida, he has been teaching for 20 years and prides himself on his versatility. His rep in the region is that he can play *anything*!

When it comes to guitars, we wrote the book

How to Play Guitar
The Basics & Beyond—Chords, Scales, Tunes & Tips
By the Editors of Guitar Player

For anyone learning to play acoustic or electric guitar, this book and CD set is packed with music, licks, and lessons from the pros. The CD guides readers through nine lessons. *Softcover, 80 pp, 8-1/2 x 11, ISBN 0-87930-399-9, $14.95*

Hot Guitar
Rock Soloing, Blues Power, Rapid-Fire Rockabilly, Slick Turnarounds, and Cool Licks • By Arlen Roth

This collection of hot techniques and cool licks includes detailed instruction and hundreds of musical examples. Drawing on ten years of the "Hot Guitar" column from *Guitar Player*, this book covers string bending, slides, picking and fingering techniques, soloing, and rock, blues, and country licks. *Softcover, 160pp, 8-1/2 x 11, ISBN 0-87930-276-3, $19.95*

Guitar Player Repair Guide
How to Set Up, Maintain, and Repair Electrics and Acoustics
By Dan Erlewine—Second Edition

Whether you're a player, collector, or repairperson, this hands-on guide provides all the essential information on caring for guitars and electric basses. Includes hundreds of photos and drawings detailing techniques for guitar care and repair. *Softcover, 309pp, 8-1/2 x 11, ISBN 0-87930-291-7, $22.95*

Picks! The Colorful Saga of Vintage Celluloid Guitar Plectrums
By Will Hoover

An eye-catching look back at the vast variety and fascinating history of vintage celluloid guitar picks. "Will Hoover has taken what you might imagine to be a mundane subject and made it fascinating." —*Billboard*
Softcover, 107pp, 6-1/2 x 6-1/2, ISBN 0-87930-377-8, $12.95

Do-It-Yourself Projects for Guitarists
35 Useful, Inexpensive Electronic Projects to Help Unlock Your Instrument's Potential
By Craig Anderton

A step-by-step guide for electric guitarists who want to create maximum personalized sound with minimum electronic problems, and get the satisfaction of achieving all this themselves. *Softcover, 176pp, 7-3/8 x 10-7/8, ISBN 0-87930-359-X, $19.95*

The Musician's Guide to Reading & Writing Music
By Dave Stewart

For the brand new rocker, the seasoned player or the pro who could use new problem-solving methods, this is a clear and practical guide to learning written music notation. "Essential reading for hitherto lazy rock musicians!" —*Keyboard*
Softcover, 112pp, 6 x 9, ISBN 0-87930-273-9, $9.95

The Musician's Home Recording Handbook
Practical Techniques for Recording Great Music at Home
By Ted Greenwald

This easy-to-follow, practical guide to setting up a home recording studio will help any musician who wants to get the best results from the equipment already at hand. *Softcover, 176pp, 8-1/2 x 11, ISBN 0-87930-237-2, $19.95*

Jaco • The Extraordinary and Tragic Life of Jaco Pastorius, "The World's Greatest Bass Player"
By Bill Milkowski

This is a fitting tribute to the talented but tormented genius who revolutionized the electric bass and single-handedly fused jazz, classical, R&B, rock, reggae, pop, and punk—all before the age of 35, when he met his tragic death. *Hardcover, 264pp, 6 x 9, ISBN 0-87930-361-1, $22.95*

Secrets from the Masters • 40 Great Guitar Players
Edited by Don Menn

Featuring the most influential guitarists of the past 25 years: Jimi Hendrix, Les Paul, Eric Clapton, Eddie Van Halen, Chuck Berry, Andrés Segovia, Pete Townshend and many more. Combines personal biography, career history, and playing techniques. *Softcover, 300 pp, 8-1/2 x 11, ISBN 0-87930-260-7, $19.95*

Blues Guitar • The Men Who Made the Music
Second Edition • Edited by Jas Obrecht

Readers get a look inside the lives and music of thirty great bluesmen, through interviews, articles, discographies, and rare photographs. Covers Buddy Guy, Robert Johnson, John Lee Hooker, Albert King, B.B. King, Muddy Waters, and more. *Softcover, 280pp, 8-1/2 x 11, ISBN 0-87930-292-5, $19.95*

Rock Hardware
40 Years of Rock Instrumentation
by Tony Bacon

This richly illustrated book chronicles the development of the great instruments of rock, how they are used, and how they shape the sound of popular music. It covers guitars, keyboards, drums, brass, recording gear, and more. *Softcover, 144pp, 8-1/2 x 11, 200 color photos, ISBN 0-87930-428-6, $24.95*

Electric Guitars and Basses • A Photographic History
By George Gruhn and Walter Carter

This striking, full-color companion volume to Gruhn and Carter's acclaimed book on acoustics traces the technical and aesthetic development of American electric guitars and their manufacturers from 1935 to the present. *Hardcover, 256pp, 8-3/4 x 11-1/2, ISBN 0-87930-328-X, $39.95*

Acoustic Guitars And Other Fretted Instruments
By George Gruhn and Walter Carter

This lavishly illustrated book tells the complete story of American acoustic guitars, mandolins, and banjos—from the 1830s to the present. Hundreds of dazzling color photos showcase luthiers' exquisite and stunning craftsmanship. *Hardcover, 320pp, 8-3/4 x 11-1/2, ISBN 0-87930-240-2, $49.95*

The Story of the Fender Stratocaster
"Curves, Contours and Body Horns" — A Celebration of the World's Greatest Guitar
By Ray Minhinnett and Bob Young

This loving profile of the American electric guitar that gave us rock 'n' roll and changed pop culture forever features exclusive interviews and color photos of the legendary Strat, its creators, and famous players. *Hardcover, 128pp, 9-1/6 x 11, ISBN 0-87930-349-2, $24.95*

Gibson's Fabulous Flat-Top Guitars
By Eldon Whitford, David Vinopal, and Dan Erlewine

250 photos and detailed text illustrate the development of Gibson's flat-tops, showing why these guitars have been the choice of so many great musicians over the decades. Includes detailed specs on historic and modern Gibson flat-tops. *Softcover, 207pp, 8-1/2 x 11, ISBN 0-87930-297-6, $22.95*

Gruhn's Guide to Vintage Guitars
An Identification Guide for American Fretted Instruments
By George Gruhn and Walter Carter

This portable reference for identifying American guitars, mandolins, and basses provides comprehensive dating information and model specifications for nearly 2,000 instruments made by all major U.S. manufacturers. For collectors, dealers, players, and fans. *Hardcover, 384pp, 4 x 7-1/2, ISBN 0-87930-195-3, $22.95*

The Art of Inlay • Contemporary Design & Technique
By Larry Robinson

This is a dazzling, full-color celebration of both the magical art of inlay and a hands-on guide to its endless creative potential. Includes 70 photos of exquisitely inlaid guitars, banjos, mandolins and various objets d'art, plus how-to instructions. *Hardcover, 112pp, 7-1/2 x 9-1/2, ISBN 0-87930-332-8, $24.95*

Fender: The Inside Story
By Forrest White

As Leo Fender always wanted, here's the story of the Fender Electric Instrument Co. "just the way it happened." His friend and only general manager traces the company's history, from Leo's start as a radio repairman through the sale to CBS, and beyond. *Softcover, 272pp, 7-3/8 x 9-1/4, ISBN 0-87930-309-3, $22.95*

The Fender Book • A Complete History of Fender Electric Guitars
By Tony Bacon and Paul Day

This is the fascinating story of Fender electric guitars, from the classic 1950s Telecaster and Stratocaster to current models. The genius of Leo Fender comes to life through unique color photos of outstanding Fender models. *Hardcover, 96pp, 7-1/2 x 9-3/4, ISBN 0-87930-259-3, $19.95*

All Music Guide to Rock
The Best CDs, Albums & Tapes—Rock, Pop, Soul, R&B, and Rap • Edited by Michael Erlewine, et. al.

This is the ultimate guide to rock recordings. For 15,500 CDs, albums and tapes by 2,500 artists—everything from doo-wop to hip-hop—you get concise reviews, expert ratings and revealing career profiles, plus historical music maps and dozens of essays on rock styles and influences. *Softcover, 970pp, 6-1/8 x 9-1/4, ISBN 0-87930-376-X, $24.95*

From the Publishers of
GuitarPlayer ®

Miller Freeman Books

Available at fine book and music stores, or contact:	**Miller Freeman Books** , 6600 Silacci Way, Gilroy, CA 95020
	Phone (800) 848-5594 • Fax (408) 848-5784
	E-Mail: mfbooks@mfi.com • http://wwwbooks.mfi.com